# GETTING *UP!*

# Getting UP!

## SUPERCHARGING YOUR ENERGY

## Greg Conderacci

**Good Ground Consulting LLC**
Baltimore, Maryland

**www.MorePersonalEnergy.com**

Cover design by Cathy Evans, Shoot the Moon

Book design by Sensical Design & Communication

PRINTED IN THE UNITED STATES OF AMERICA

*To my mother, Mary,*
*My first energy buddy.*
*And my father, Fred,*
*Who taught me to*
*"Run my own race."*

# Thank YOU!

— — — — — — — — — — — — — — — — —

MANY THANKS TO ALL THE ENERGY BUDDIES THAT HELPED MAKE this book possible and who shared their support, insights and wisdom, including:

- ⚡ Bob Brosmer

- ⚡ Chuck Camp

- ⚡ Anthony Davis

- ⚡ Sara Eisenberg

- ⚡ Cathy Evans

- ⚡ John Fuoco

- ⚡ Jim Gabriel

- ⚡ Maggi Gaines

- ⚡ Barbara Hill

- ⚡ Daniel Kohan

- ⚡ Andrea Matney

- ⚡ Joe Mechlinski

- ⚡ Tom Steinert-Threlkeld

- ⚡ Hal Smith

- ⚡ Frank Ryan

# Table of Contents

## Part Seven: Moving Toward a More Balanced, Happier Life

## Appendices

# Energy-Saving Introduction

Don't you hate long introductions?

Me, too.

Want supercharged energy to do amazing things? To reduce stress? To restore balance to your life?

Read on.

# PART ONE

# Why Energy Is More Important Than Time

# 1

# The "Bad Morning" Energy Crisis

— — — — — — — — — — — — — —

**"I wake up so excited I can't eat breakfast. I've never run out of energy. It's not like OPEC oil; I don't worry about a premium going on my energy. It's just always been there. I got it from my mom." —Steven Spielberg**

— — — — — — — — — — — — — —

DAWN. LAP 17. SIXTY MILES TO GO.

Beneath me, the bicycle hums contentedly over the Texas tar-and-chip, just as it has for the last 35 hours. It was made for this. And so am I. In the rosy silence of the morning, the high-energy voice in my head rejoices:

"Light. Good! It will be easier now, in the light. You will make it."

But the low-energy voice worries:

"You've ridden 440 miles in a day and a half. Aren't you running a little low on juice, Old Timer?" A few hours ago, in the gloom of the night, I had given in to this voice. I had stopped, begging a volunteer to allow me a few precious moments sleep in the back of his car.

But now, I see a competitor ahead, a mere speck in the morning sun, struggling a bit on a hill. Like an old CB radio, the first voice crackles:

"I am Bright Hawk. And you, little birdie, are *mine*."

Suddenly, the distance, the sleep depravation, and the discomfort of a well-worn saddle no longer matter. I will catch this rider. I will pass him. Like a patient raptor watching a mouse inch across a field, I lock onto this rider. Accelerating, I stretch out in the cockpit, savoring the surge of energy, clawing closer.

Suddenly, I am at his side. Clearly, he is tired, feeling the strain. I roll by, effortlessly. He does not respond.

There's no stopping me now. I am threading my way through the dusty Texas scrub to my dream.

The bike seems to barely touch the ground as the final miles melt away in the shimmering September heat. My time for the 19th and final 26-mile lap is almost as fast as my first. I roll over the finish line of the 2011 Texas Time Trials, riding 500 miles in 39 hours and 53 minutes. In that time, I have climbed a total of 30,000 feet—the height of Everest. At the ripe old age of 62, I have qualified for Race Across America, the cycling equivalent of a marathoner qualifying for Boston.

## But on a Normal Day...

Somewhere, someone gets up in the morning refreshed and full of energy. She powers through the day, accomplishing five times as much as her lackluster peers. She leaves stress far behind, leading a magnificently balanced life as a top executive, community leader, mother, spouse and athlete.

> **We suffer from the most widespread energy crisis in history.**

...And then there's you, me and the rest of the world. We suffer from the most widespread energy crisis in history. It has nothing to do with oil, gas or solar power. It's...it's...*it's hard to get up in the morning.*

Indeed, it's hard to get up—period—for a lot of what we must do.[1] We used to think we didn't have enough time, but the ugly truth is we just don't have enough energy.

The good news is that we can *get* more energy. The bad news is that the ways we get it are often expensive, dangerous and counterproductive. There are better ways.

This book is about a different approach toward getting *UP*—the energy to be ready, willing and able to live the successful, balanced life you want. Like the folks in my energy seminars, you'll learn why:

⚡ Managing your energy, *not* your time, is the secret;

⚡ Getting more energy isn't about what you drink...it's about what you *think*;

⚡ Driving a stake through the hearts of the *vampires* sucking your life away might help;

⚡ Supercharging your energy is *inexpensive, simple and fun.*

## EnergyThink: Will You Give It a Try?

There are two kinds of consultants: answer consultants and question consultants. I am the latter. At the end of every chapter, I'll leave you with some questions to help you get *UP* in every area of your life. I hope they resonate with you.

So, in a world crazy for energy drinks, this is just a sip of EnergyTHINK. No (Red) Bull.

⚡ Do you want more energy? What kind do you need … especially?

⚡ Do you want a happier, fuller life? What does that mean for you?

# 2

# My Getting *UP* "Chops"

---

**"I thought of it while riding my bicycle."
—Albert Einstein, on the Theory of Relativity**

---

"WHO ARE YOU TO WRITE ABOUT ENERGY?" WOULD BE A PERFECTLY GOOD question for you to ask.

I am *not*:

⚡ An Olympic gold medalist;

⚡ A coach of Olympic gold medalist;

⚡ A promoter who has hired a coach of an Olympic gold medalist to sell diet supplements, exercise equipment and yoga vacations.

I am like *you*:

⚡ Not as young as I used to be;

⚡ Dealing with the stress of too much to do and too little time to do it;

⚡ Striving to bring balance to a demanding life and career.

One difference between us is that I probably have way more energy than you do. And I'd like to tell you how you can get more energy yourself—so you can do amazing things, better manage stress, and improve balance in your life. As I have told thousands of others in my energy seminars, you don't have to be Einstein to figure this out (although there is a lot of wisdom in this book from a lot of people a lot smarter than I am). *And you don't have to buy anything.*

THE QUESTION "WHO ARE YOU TO WRITE ABOUT ENERGY?" FLICKED through my mind as I stood in a San Diego motel parking lot in May 2015, working hard on Getting UP. Fifteen other cycling lunatics and I were set to embark on Elite PAC Tour.

Humbly promoting itself as "The Toughest Two-Week Bicycle Tour in the World," Elite PAC is the brainchild of Lon Haldeman and Susan Notorangelo, two former Race Across America champions and holders of coast-to-coast cycling records. The pair's company, PAC Tour, has shepherded more than 80 rides across America over three decades.

Elite PAC is a 2,700-mile-plus dash from San Diego, California to Savannah, Georgia in just 18 days—or an average of about 150 miles a day. Designed for the strongest and most manic distance riders, it is not for the faint of heart. Short of Race Across America itself, it is the ultimate test of a road bike rider's cross-country energy and endurance.

> **Life imitates riding across the country.**

The United States is a big country, full of mountains, deserts, endless farms and un-remitting tar-and-chip-covered rough roads. It demands UP over and over again. To ride Elite PAC, I would have to work at Getting UP every time I got side-swiped by a speeding logging truck and in every pelting rain storm. I had to Get UP to fight blast-furnace headwinds and to nurse my rickety knees over saw-tooth hills.

## Life Imitates Long Distance Cycling

PAC Tour is a great way to spend 18 days...if you're planning to write a book on energy...because *life imitates riding across the country.* Just ask Einstein, who knew a bit about energy. He said, "Life is like riding a bicycle. To keep your balance, you must keep moving." And, on PAC Tour...

⚡ Each day brings its own challenges;

⚡ The external obstacles, like mountains and traffic, are unchanging and uncaring;

⚡ The internal obstacles are tougher: pain, exhaustion, anxiety, confusion, discouragement, irritation, distraction;

⚡ Sometimes, you ride with friends; sometimes, you must ride alone;

⚡ You must decide how to spend your energy; how to save it; how to recover it;

⚡ It's a little dangerous;

⚡ Tomorrow, you ride again.[1]

At 66, Medicare card in my wallet, I became the oldest rider to complete this event since it began in 1995. Some folks think it's pretty impressive that an old fart like me could ride that long and hard. In this book and my courses, I'm going to argue that it's no big deal compared to the amazing things YOU could do with more energy.

## The Difference a Decade of Distance Makes

It wasn't my first trip across the country on a bike. I had done it with the PAC Tour folks before, in 2004, amid a torrent of transition in my life. Hard at work on a mid-life crisis, I was leaving my wife of more than two decades, trying to establish a consulting firm, moving one daughter out of college and another in, and hoping to raise money for my favorite charity.

Stressful? You bet.

Then, riding from Seattle, Washington to Williamsburg, Virginia in 26 days was the immediate challenge, but not the only one. I would need a lot of energy in 2004 and for every year after that for a long list of challenges.

Between the two cross-country trips, I have:

⚡ Twice completed the world's oldest bicycle race, Paris-Brest-Paris, a 750-mile, no-time-out haul from Paris to the Atlantic Ocean and back;

⚡ Qualified for Race Across America twice;

⚡ Climbed Mount Kilimanjaro, the highest mountain in Africa;

⚡ Raced 1,000 miles around Italy in about five days, climbing 60,000 feet (twice the height of Everest);

⚡ Ridden in many other events, often riding more than 200 miles a day.

AND...

⚡ Re-built a wonderful friendship with my former spouse, who is a great person;

⚡ Saw my two children graduate from prestigious colleges and go on to good careers;

⚡ Successfully grew my consulting practice, providing marketing advice to scores of organizations and training hundreds of executives, professionals and salespeople;

⚡ Became an associate faculty member at the Johns Hopkins Bloomberg School of Public Health, teaching grad students how to market health care organizations;

⚡ Spent a lot of time training people on how to boost and manage their personal energy. I've spoken to groups at Prudential, MetLife, Wells Fargo, McCormick (the big spice company), Dollar Tree, Catholic Charities, the YMCA, and a host of others. I've worked with both non-profits and for-profits, from salespeople to CPAs to CEOs, all over the country. (For more information, see my website: www. MorePersonalEnergy.com.)

> **What could you do if you had that much energy?**

This really *isn't* a book about bicycling. To quote the infamous Lance Armstrong, "It's not about the bike." It's about energy and how boosting it can rebalance your life and push back the stress. The bicycle is just the test bed—and the "proof"—for what I'm advocating. The bike is a machine that goes nowhere without energy and balance—just like our lives. This book is a little autobiographical. But it's not about me as much as it is about you (or at least *us*).

Look at it this way: you can ride a bike, too. When you strip everything away, riding across the country is just pedal, pedal, pedal—about a million pedal turns. So the only real difference between you and me is that I have the energy to ride coast-to-coast and you don't...*yet*.

What could you do if you had that much energy? Could you rebalance an unbalanced life?

Throughout my life, I've been mostly *living* myself into thinking differently—not thinking myself into living differently. The energy and endurance lessons that I learned over the years have helped me with every challenge I've faced.

I hope they work for you, too.

## EnergyThink: The Power of Midrash

The Jewish practice of *midrash* involves asking questions, rather than seeking immediate answers, about scripture. It broadens thinking, opening many possibilities. It's a good practice to apply to our lives. So, don't worry if you don't have immediate answers to many of the "EnergyThinks" in this book.

German poet Rainer Maria Rilke has some good advice on this: "Have patience with everything that remains unsolved in your heart. Try to love the *questions themselves*, like locked rooms and like books written in a foreign language. Do not now look for the answers. They cannot now be given to you because you could not live them. It is a question of experiencing everything. At present you need to *live* the question. Perhaps you will gradually, without even noticing it, find yourself experiencing the answer, some distant day."[2]

Just a couple of simple questions to live with:

⚡ Where is your life out of balance? Why? (It's okay: we're all at least a little off kilter.)

⚡ If you got your balance back or better, what would you want to do?

# 3

# The Seven Secrets of Supercharging

"It's not whether you get knocked down. It's whether
you get up again." —Coach Vince Lombardi

ARE YOU *UP*?

This is a book about Getting *UP*. *UP* is having the *energy* to be ready,
willing and able to take on a challenge. All of us need to get *UP*.

Getting *UP* when we're knocked down. Getting *UP* in the morning.
Getting the team *UP* for the game. Getting *UP* to change careers, mates,
lifestyles, houses, cities, and the way we load the toilet paper. Even getting
*UP* for sex (which is a major industry, if you haven't noticed).

Are you *UP* for Getting *UP*? You will need to be *UP* when:

⚡ You find out your father has Alzheimer's;

⚡ Your cruise ship sinks and you have no drinking water on the rubber
raft;

⚡ You have two more miles to go in the half marathon;

⚡ You tell off that bully of a boss (and you need to find another job);

⚡ You confront the slings and arrows of outrageous fortune, the sea of
troubles, the heartache and the thousand natural shocks that flesh is
heir to (to borrow a line from Hamlet).

Getting *UP* can save your life literally (as in the raft example) and also
help save your life from poverty, stress, boredom and ignorance…just
for starters. Often, we face challenges that demand more energy than we
think we have. We need *supercharged* energy. On an engine, a supercharger
crams in extra fuel and oxygen, dramatically increasing power. You can

do it, too, if you know *The Seven Supercharging Secrets of Getting UP*. The first two seem obvious, but you'd never know it from most folks' "normal" behavior:

1. You can't get any more time in a day, but you can get more energy.

2. Energy is more important than time.

The next four are all about the four different but related types of energy (I remember them with the acronym PIES):

3. **Physical energy** is fuel-driven; it's about food and sleep.

4. **Intellectual energy** is story-driven; it's about your ideas and beliefs.

5. **Emotional energy** is mood-driven; it's about your feelings and fears.

6. **Spiritual energy** is mission-driven; it's about your identity and values.

And the last one brings everything together: it may be the reason you're reading this book. It's what you need the energy for. It's how you ultimately get what you want:

7. The secret of a more powerful, balanced, happy life is using your energy to live your mission.

It looks a lot like Illustration #1.

Are you *UP* for thinking about that for a minute?

**1. You can't get any more time in a day, but you can get more energy.** Since time is limited (just 24 hours per day), it's good news that we can get more energy. Here are some obvious ways:

⚡ You eat a candy bar on your coffee break;

⚡ You hire somebody to help you move into your new house (in theory, twice the energy);

⚡ You get a really good night's sleep (remember you did that once?);

⚡ You plumb the depths of your being and draw upon vast amounts of spiritual energy.

Duh, right?

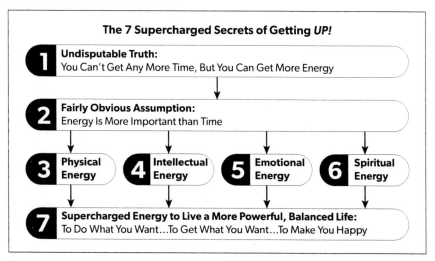

*Illustration #1: Rebalancing your life demands a shift in focus toward energy and away from time. You have to be able to tap all four pools of energy within to reduce stress, reach your goals and find the happiness you want.*

**2. Energy is more important than time.** Obviously, meeting any challenge takes both time and energy. But if you're *UP* for doing something, it's probably going to take a lot less time than if you're not:

⚡ Are you *UP* for writing that "thank you" note?

⚡ Are you *UP* for cleaning the bathroom?

⚡ Are you *UP* for that difficult conversation with your neighbor?

⚡ Are you *UP* to make the next sales call?

See what I mean?

**3. Physical energy is fuel-driven; it's about food and sleep.** So, getting more physical energy for our bodies, something many people are obsessed with, can be relatively straightforward. Are you tired? Low on energy?

⚡ Eat;

⚡ Sleep;

⚡ Exercise;

⚡ Take drugs.

*Oops.* I almost forgot to tell you about this increasingly popular last option, especially if you want to win the Tour de France.

**4. Intellectual energy is story-driven; it's about your ideas and beliefs.** Motivational speaker Brian Tracey has a great line about this: "You are *not* what you think you are, but what you think, you *are.*" All of us have thousands of stories rattling around in our heads shaping our experience and our energy. For example:

⚡ The right way to mount toilet tissue;

⚡ Why your home team is better than mine;

⚡ "Because I'm the mom, that's why";

⚡ "Because that's the way we do it here."

"We do not see the world as it is; we see the world as we are." —The Talmud.

**5. Emotional energy is mood-driven; it's about your feelings and fears.** Deep in our skulls, the primal brain lurks, teeming with all the same primitive emotions as a reptile (hence, the name, "lizard brain"). Most of the time, we aren't even conscious of its instinctive, rapid-fire decision-making power and energy. But:

⚡ The other guy intercepts the pass meant for you;

⚡ She cut in line in front of you at the movie theater;

⚡ Those shoes you've be lusting after just went on sale;

⚡ There is a conspiracy to take away your guns.

It's why the Internet is flooded with pornography.

**6. Spiritual energy is mission-driven; it's about your identity and values.** Mark Twain once said that the two best days of your life are the day you're born and the day you find out why. You get a lot of extra juice over a longer period of time if you know:

⚡ Who you are;

⚡ What your purpose in life is;

⚡ Your values;

⚡ How to live them.

Just think of any world leader who left behind a lasting impact.

**7. The secret of "Getting *UP*" for a more powerful, balanced, happy life is using your energy to live your mission.** In the end, it's how you do what you want to do and get what you want to get. You might be wondering:

⚡ What's a mission?

⚡ Why would you want one?

⚡ How do you get one?

⚡ What would you do with it?

We'll get to all that before this is over.

## EnergyThink: What Do You Need to Get *UP* For?

Every self-help author says his or her book will change your life. This book will *not* change your life. YOU will change your life.

⚡ Are you willing to invest a little precious time reading these few pages—in the hope you'll figure out a way to do that?

⚡ If you have any medical issues, be sure to consult a health care professional before undertaking any exercise program.

⚡ You have to use your judgment. I am not a physician (although I do teach them marketing!) and I don't give medical advice. Or, as the lawyers like to say, *this book is not designed to and does not provide medical advice, professional diagnosis, opinion, treatment or services. Medical information provided is for informational and educational purposes only. After reading this book, you should review the information carefully with your physician. Never disregard professional medical advice, delay in seeking treatment, or rely on the information contained on this book in place of seeking professional medical advice. Medical information changes constantly and I can't guarantee the accuracy, adequacy, timeliness or completeness of any of the information.*

# 5

# Getting Over The Lie of Time

— — — — — — — — — — — — — — —

**"All my possessions for a moment of time."**
**—Last words of Queen Elizabeth I of England**

— — — — — — — — — — — — — — —

DON'T WORRY ABOUT CHAPTER FOUR. THE POINT IS THAT YOU'RE FIVE chapters in and you've only been reading a few minutes. *You are way ahead of schedule.* If that sounds crazy, but a little familiar, it's because we've all bought into the Lie of Time.

An important part of Getting *UP* is *getting over* the Lie of Time.

Why are we so obsessed with time? My theory: We have all been fed a time "line" from infancy:

⚡ All time is sacred;

⚡ Make every second count;

⚡ Invest time in what we care about most;

⚡ Do that, and your life will have meaning and your relationships will grow.

So we spend "quality time" with our kids. We cram every spare moment with activity, even if it's just texting or checking email. We are terrified of "wasting time." Standing in line, stuck in traffic, during half-time at the kids' soccer matches, we are moved almost to distraction as we watch our lives slipping away, second by second. And we skip important things. Like Chapter Four.

Where did we get this foolishness? Well, it goes back a couple hundred years to the dawn of the Industrial Revolution. On an assembly line, time *is* money. Line moves ... you're making money. Line stops...you're "wasting time" and losing money. These ideas don't apply much any more because it's the 21st Century, for Pete's sake. Do *you* work on an assembly line?

## No Help from School

Of course, that doesn't stop our educational system from grinding away with an "old school" mentality. (A major frustration for a teacher and trainer like me.) Even though few of us work on assembly lines today, two centuries later our schools are still teaching our kids to:

⚡ Show up on time;

⚡ Learn their lessons, with an emphasis on memory;

⚡ Pay attention constantly;

⚡ Do exactly what they are told;

⚡ Ask no questions;

⚡ Waste not a moment.

> **Have you ever taken a time management course? Did it change your life?**

*If you don't have enough time, you need to be a better time manager…* it's what all the time management courses say. Have you ever taken a time management course? Did it change your life? Time management isn't bad, but after you get organized, what then? That's why I teach *Energy* Management, *not* time management.

Are you *UP* for an extra three or four hours a day? Okay, here are my "time management" secrets, which involve little more than dumping the big time suckers:

⚡ Don't watch television

⚡ Shorten your commute

⚡ Get off Facebook and other social media

⚡ Never go to BuzzFeed or Reddit

⚡ Check email only four times a day

⚡ Demand agendas for all your business meetings

⚡ Never touch a piece of paper or an email more than once

- ⚡ Unsubscribe to all commercial email (like Groupon and Angie's List)

- ⚡ Never play video games.

I know. I know. Radical stuff. But now you know how badly you want those extra hours. Research firm Analysys Mason estimated that the average smart phone owner spends 195 minutes a day on the device—3 hours and 15 minutes![1]

The *good* new is that many of the so-called "time wasters" can actually be energy builders. For example, if an hour on BuzzFeed or Facebook relaxes you, inspires some great ideas and improves your outlook on life, then maybe it's a good investment from an energy standpoint. And that goes for other so-called "time wasters" like fishing, taking naps in the afternoon, watching sunrises and sets, and channel surfing.

> **The average smart phone owner spends 195 minutes a day on the device.**

A friend of mine, financial adviser, author and blogger Tim Mauer, wrote that his son gave him a chunk of pyrite, AKA "fool's gold." He says it's "a constant reminder to orient my life away from that which only *appears* valuable and towards that which truly is." How can you recognize the "fool's gold" in your life? He writes:

- ⚡ Fool's gold consumes time you've dedicated to other things;

- ⚡ Fool's gold leaves you wanting more, but still dissatisfied;

- ⚡ Fool's gold steals attention from the genuine treasures in your life.[2]

## Time to Smell the Red Bull?

Look: if Albert Einstein came back from the dead with an explanation of how the universe fits together, he would probably get fewer "likes" than a cat video. Can you *believe* what you watch online? Isn't playing games on your smart phone about as satisfying as scratching poison ivy? The philosopher Kierkegaard warned against "tranquilization by the trivial." Isn't that our story?

Much of what is valuable today doesn't depend on time. How long does it take to discover a cure for cancer? To write the great American novel? To come up with that breakthrough idea at work? To make an associate feel appreciated? To stand up for what you believe? To even figure out what that is?

You can't get more time. And time *is* valuable. But what if the game is really about energy?

Get *UP* and smell the Red Bull.[3] The 21st Century is about energy. So hang in there. There's plenty of time.

## EnergyThink: Are You *UP* for Getting Beyond the Lie of Time?

"Ninety percent of the game is half mental," Yogi Berra said. Getting beyond the lie of time is *all* mental:

- ⚡ Does your focus on time actually slow you down? How?

- ⚡ Do you waste valuable energy worrying about how you're "wasting" time?

- ⚡ For example, how do you feel if you "miss" a green light and have to wait through another cycle at the intersection? Is that a "good" feeling or a "bad" one?

- ⚡ Because of your focus on time, what are you missing?

# 6

## Selling Your Soul for More *UP*

— — — — — — — — — — — — — — —

**"Everybody wants to know what I'm on. What am I on? I'm on my bike, busting my ass six hours a day. What are you on?" —Lance Armstrong, Nike Commercial, 2001**

— — — — — — — — — — — — — — —

SPEAKING OF BICYCLE RIDERS, IT IS NOW TIME TO TAKE UP THE CASE of Lance Edward Armstrong. Liar. Cheat. Bully. Sure. But you clip that boy onto his Trek and he was like no other. Who cares if he has an extra quart of blood, a few designer hormones and a drug made for cancer victims? After all, he *was* a cancer victim.

Turns out, of course, a lot of people do care. In my energy courses, I love running his famous Nike commercial where he claims he was on his bike, "busting my ass six hours a day." That was, well, partially true...

In October 2012, the U.S. Anti-Doping Agency said his U.S. Postal Service team "ran the most sophisticated, professionalized and successful doping program that sport has ever seen." Armstrong lost his seven Tour de France titles. (Now, there are officially no winners for those seven years, since nobody knows what the *other* guys were taking but them.)

*I care, too....but for somewhat different reasons. Lance stands at an historic pivot point:* **the greatest athlete with the best pharmacy.** *He is the poster child for the all-out, 21st Century stampede to get more energy, by any means available.*

The mad rush for more juice is the impetus behind Starbucks, Red Bull, and a host of other pills and potions that have become a multi-billion-dollar world-wide market. According to the website Statistica, sales of energy drink beverages in the U.S. topped $10 billion in 2013 and will reach an estimated $13.5 billion in 2015.[1] The CaffeineInformer.com website says that industry leader Red Bull's global sales were almost $11 billion in 2013.[2]

That's a lot of money for a drink that tastes like cough syrup. Only God and Lance know for sure what he paid in cash for his energy. In a more costly calculus, he paid with his integrity.

## Inside Lance's Bloodstream...

A little caffeine doesn't even begin to describe what could have been coursing through his veins:

⚡ **Anabolic steroids, such as testosterone:** Used to increase muscle mass, they also can help athletes recover more quickly from exertion. Side effects include: acne, baldness, liver damage, high blood pressure, depression, heart and circulatory problems, increased aggression and sexual desire, and in men, impotence, breast-tissue development, shrinking of the testicles and reduction in sperm production.

⚡ **Human growth hormone (HGH):** May help athletes build muscle mass and perform better. Side effects: diabetes, allergic reactions, joint pain, muscle weakness, cardio-myopathy, high cholesterol and hypertension.

> Lance stands at an historic pivot point: the greatest athlete with the best pharmacy.

⚡ **Erythropoietin (EPO):** Stimulates red blood cell production, improving the amount of oxygen the blood can deliver to muscles, giving athletes more endurance. Side effects: higher risk of stroke, heart attack and pulmonary edema. It is said to have contributed to the deaths of 18 competitive cyclists in the 1990s.

⚡ **Blood transfusions/blood doping:** This involves removing an athlete's own blood before competition, and then re-injecting that blood right before a competition or during the event. Doing so gives the athlete a boost in red blood cells, and improves the amount of oxygen the blood can deliver to muscles. That helps athletes with endurance and recovery after exertion. Side effects: increased risk of heart attack, stroke, and pulmonary or brain embolism.

⚡ **Cortisone:** It's a steroid, but not like anabolic steroids, such as testosterone. Cortisone reduces inflammation, pain and swelling. Side effects:

increased appetite, indigestion, nervousness, blurred vision, frequent urination, increased thirst, mood swings, flushing of the face or cheeks, increased susceptibility to infection, stomach ulcers and depression, among other effects.[3]

Not long ago, British Broadcasting asked Lance, if he had it to do all over again, would he still cheat? His answer: yes.[4] He's lost his balance.

## EnergyThink: What Would You Do for More Energy?

Put yourself in Lance's cycling shoes.

⚡ Would you do it? Would you take the drugs? If you do, there is the promise of fame and fortune. You are a global inspiration, a champion who fought The Big C and the best cyclists in the world (many of whom were probably taking the same drugs you did).

⚡ Perhaps, for you and me, it's easy to look back and say, "I would *never* do that." But you can understand the temptation, can't you?

⚡ Do you recognize it in yourself in that late-night cup of coffee that will keep you up a little longer working on that important project due tomorrow?

⚡ Do you see it in that energy drink you're sipping to help you keep up with "the kids"?

# PART TWO

# How You Can Get More Energy

# 7

# Getting *UP* While Getting Older

---

**"No wise person ever wanted to be younger." —Native American Aphorism**

---

TICK TOCK.

Speaking of time, are you feeling a little older these days?

My energy "poster child" is Robert Marchand, who in early 2014 set a new world age-group record of 16.7 miles for an hour ride on a bicycle. If that doesn't sound too impressive, consider that Mr. Marchand's "age group" is "over 100." He was 102 and he broke his old record set when he was 100.[1] Still think you're too old?

How about this? In January 2015, *The Journal of Physiology*[2] published a study of recreational cyclists aged 55 to 79 that showed their performance was remarkably similar to much younger people.

"We wanted to understand what happens to the functioning of our bodies as we get older if we take the best-case scenario," Stephen Harridge, senior author of the study and director of the Centre of Human and Aerospace Physiological Sciences at King's College London, told *The New York Times*.[3] So they picked 85 men and 41 women who rode regularly, but who weren't elite athletes, and studied their physical and mental performance.

"As it turned out, the cyclists did not show their age," the *Times* reported, "On almost all measures, their physical functioning remained fairly stable across the decades and was much closer to that of young adults than of people their age. As a group, even the oldest cyclists had younger people's levels of balance, reflexes, metabolic health and memory ability."

"If you gave this dataset to a clinician and asked him to predict the age" of one of the cyclists based on his or her test results, Dr. Harridge said, "it would be impossible." *On paper, they all look young.*

## Teens vs. Mid-Lifers

There's more. In a study at Camilo Jose Cela University in Spain, researchers analyzed the mean marathon race times of more than 45,000 runners
in the New York City Marathon in 2010 and 2011.[4] They compared ages
and finishing times and noticed that on average runners' times improved
about 4% a year from their late teens to their late 20s, when they peaked.
After that, the times slowed gradually as the runners aged. *The surprise was
that runners in their late 50s were averaging about the same times as runners
in their late teens.*

In another study of marathoners published in 2014 in *BMC Sports
Science, Medicine and Rehabilitation*, researchers looked at marathon records by age—from five years old to 93.[5] For elite marathoners, the report
concluded, "the age-related loss in running performance did not occur
before the age of ~50 years. Mean marathoners race times were nearly
identical for age group runners from 20 to 49 years. Also for 100-km
ultra-marathoners, the fastest race times were observed during the age
span of 30–49 years for men and 30–54 years for women, respectively."

> **The bottom line: how
> old you are makes
> little difference…
> in the long run.**

The bottom line: how old you are makes little difference…in the long
run.

Don't we all start slowing down as we get older? It's a common question
in all my energy seminars. Yes, but not nearly as quickly or as much as the
conventional wisdom suggests. Nor do we necessarily slow down mentally
or spiritually when we slow physically. You can keep on keeping on at a
high energy level *a lot longer* than you might have thought.

## EnergyThink: Are You Ready to *Act* Old?

⚡ Notice that I didn't ask, "Are you ready to BE old?" We have no real
choice about that; it beats the alternative.

⚡ Think about what you believe to be age-appropriate behavior for you.
Then, subtract 10, 20 or 30 years. What would you do if you were
younger? Why aren't you doing that *now*?

# 8

# The Rhythm Method: When Are You *UP*?

— — — — — — — — — — — — — — —

**"It is a very good plan every now and then to go away and have a little relaxation... When you come back to work, your judgment will be surer, since to remain constantly at work will cause you to lose the power of judgment." —Leonardo da Vinci, Treatise on Painting**

— — — — — — — — — — — — — — —

ONE OF THE CHIEF "LIES OF TIME" PERPETRATED BY OUR EDUCATIONAL system is that every hour is created equal. In school, you are expected to pay just as much attention to spelling at 2 pm as you do to math at 9 am.

Putting aside the fact that I didn't like either of those subjects and didn't pay attention anyway, I discovered at an early age that I was usually a little better in the morning than in the afternoon. Of course, on an assembly line, this behavior just would not do. Which is why school tries to break us of all such patterns.

Leonardo knew better, even 400 years ago. We are rhythmic beings. For each of us, there is a better time of the day, of the week, of the year. Smart energy managers adjust their work so that the items that demand the most energy happen in high energy times. In short, it's not just about time; it's about *timing*.

For example, I was, in scientific parlance, an "early chronotype," but I didn't know it. My natural pattern looks a lot like Illustration #2. Not surprisingly, my best high school track races were on Saturday mornings and not in the afternoon during the school week.

For most of my journalistic career, I worked for a morning newspaper, *The Wall Street Journal*. Deadline was 5 pm. Afternoons were prime interviewing time, since many of my sources were a little tired (and, in the days of the two-martini lunch, well lubricated). They would talk more freely than first thing in the morning, when they were busy with the tasks of the day, fresh and (sometimes) on guard.

But, for me, it was a real struggle to write and submit stories in mid-afternoon, when my energy was low. Fortunately, as the illustration shows, my energy surged a bit towards the end of the day (as it does for many of us) and I could rally for the deadline.

## What's Your Energy Pattern?

What's your energy pattern? Does it look like illustration #2? If you're a "late chronotype" (better in the evenings), draw your pattern—and adjust your workflow. A good energy manager will put mindless, low-energy tasks (like answering email) in the low-juice times of day. Times of high productivity are good for writing and meetings. Notice that almost any time in the morning is typically better than the afternoon. Do you see the little mid-morning coffee break effect? Notice the rally right before lunch and right at the end of the work day to "clean up" what's left from the day. If you have a lunch meeting to discuss business do you want to meet earlier and *then* eat? That might be more productive than trying to talk during the "crash" right after lunch.

One of the curses of being an "energy guy" is that conference planners will often intentionally schedule my presentations at low energy times because "Greg will wake everybody up." That can be difficult, but doable. I have two strategies: activity and entertainment.

When I'm doing seminars in the afternoon, especially on Fridays, the classes have to be highly interactive and participative. And they have to

> **Where does the energy come from to party on Friday night?**

be fun. It's a good time to play games and show funny videos to get folks laughing and engaged.

I teach in the Bloomberg School of Public Health at Johns Hopkins University. My time slot is a three-hour seminar on Monday nights. It's me vs. Monday night. Only Monday morning or Friday afternoon would be worse.

What's the biggest tribute my students pay me in their course evaluations?

"He made Monday nights great."

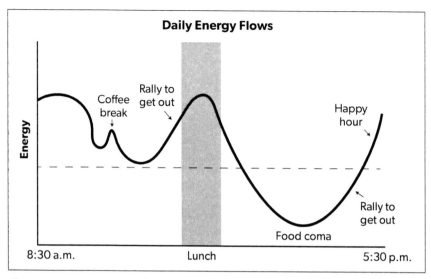

*Illustration #2: Many people find their energy is higher in the morning. This might be the pattern for an "early chronotype"—a "morning person." Manage your work to match your energy flows and you'll get more done, easier and faster. What does your pattern look like?*

## What's Your Life Like?

Here's another way to look at your energy flows. Over the course of an ultra-distance race, riders will go through several energy peaks and valleys —just like you will over a week of your life.

Sometimes, riders will be so tired they can barely move; at other times, they can be flying down the road. Both feelings can be just minutes apart. A moderation in terrain, a shift in wind, or, importantly, a change of attitude can make a dramatic difference. There's an old saying in Randon-neuring[1]: "Whether you feel great or awful...it will change." This thought has often been a consolation (when I'm feeling bad) and a caution (when I'm feeling good). Frequently, it is not the case that riders are most tired at the end, as you might expect.

Think about it: are you most tired on Friday afternoon, after a long week at work? Perhaps. But then where does the energy come from to party on Friday night?

Take a look at these six different levels of energy that riders experience. Look back over your past week. What percentage of your awake time (don't count sleep) does each level describe?

**1.** I cannot move. ___%

**2.** I can just make my way down the road, slowly. ___%

**3.** I can roll along at a steady pace. ___%

**4.** I am moving at my own pace. ___%

**5.** I am flying. ___%

**6.** I am above the road in complete flow. ___%

Ideally, you'd like to spend as much time as possible in stages 4, 5 and 6. Not all weeks will be the same, of course. But this is not a bad snapshot of your energy profile. Lance had an expression for level 6: "No chain." In other words, pedaling was so effortless it was as if there was no chain on his bike.

## EnergyThink: What Are Your Patterns?

"Life is like riding a bicycle. You don't fall off unless you plan to stop pedaling," said long-time Florida Senator Claude Pepper. Given that you plan to keep pedaling for a while, why not pedal hardest when you can go fastest? It's one secret to keeping your balance.

⚡ It would be nice to have more "no chain" time, wouldn't it?

⚡ What are your daily and weekly energy patterns? Draw yourself a couple of pictures.

⚡ Could you change your schedule to use your most productive time better? How?

# PART THREE

# Boosting Physical Energy

# 9

# PIES: Fill *UP* Your Energy "Tanks"

— — — — — — — — — — — — — —

**"What lies behind us and what lies before us are tiny matters compared to what lies within us." —Ralph Waldo Emerson**

— — — — — — — — — — — — — —

JIM LOEHR AND TONY SCHWARTZ, IN *THE POWER OF FULL ENGAGEMENT*, popularized the notion that there are essentially four major types of personal energy. I find it easy to remember them by thinking of PIES: Physical, Intellectual, Emotional and Spiritual.[1]

On an ultra-distance cycle race, I will go to each of my energy "fuel tanks" several times. If the sheer miles aren't enough to challenge the limits of endurance then there is always The Dreaded Four H's: Hills, Heat, Head winds and Humidity.

Physically, I make sure I get good sleep the night before a race (and, especially, two nights before); I drink and eat regularly; I'm careful about expending too much energy too early in the contest.

Intellectually, I *focus* on positive self talk and *avoid* thinking about how far I have yet to go; I try to stay "in the moment" and enjoy it. Emotionally, I try to ride with good friends who can help me over the inevitable "rough patches" of low energy. Positive energy generates positive energy.

Spiritually, I keep on keeping on because, well, I don't like to quit. And the ability to overcome the challenges of the road reinforces my self image. Accomplishment feels good.

During the average work week, without ever thinking about them, you probably reach into your "fuel tanks," too. What's more, you and I have been doing it, mostly unconsciously, for all of our lives.

Is it better to do it *consciously*? "To be fully engaged, we must be physically energized, emotionally connected, mentally focused and spiritually aligned," Loehr and Schwartz declared. You can see my version of this, the Supercharger Model, in Illustration #3.

Although it's useful to consider them separately, all four of these "energy tanks" *blend and merge and feed each other.* Like an airplane that relies on several fuel tanks to fly its route (and stay balanced in the air), we draw from all four. Sometimes simultaneously, sometimes more from one tank or the other. Let's look at some examples.

## Physical Energy: The Saga of the Scrub

*Physical Energy* is the most deceptively obvious, mostly because we have little idea of how much is *really* in this bucket.

My introduction to the foibles of physical energy came in freshman year of high school when I was the biggest scrub on the frosh football team. As a football player, I wasn't half bad. I was all bad. I was, in fact, pathetic.

> **Run fast. Turn left. Even I could figure that out.**

The end of the bench was my home. We finished the season with only 22 guys on the team, yet I never played a single play in any of the games. The coaches wouldn't even put me in when we were losing badly, which was all the time. What I lacked in physical strength, agility and size I more than made up for by executing knuckle-headed moves like tackling my own halfback in practice.

As a result, the coaches frequently dished out to me the most dreaded punishment they could imagine: run a mile on the track. To me, the track wasn't so terrible. I was thinking that it might even be fun if I wasn't carrying all that football armor. Even better, nobody tackled you on the track. And there were no complicated plays to screw up or balls to fumble. Run fast. Turn left. Even I could figure that out.

In the spring, I went out for track, much to the relief of my parents who had grown tired of replacing the caps on my front teeth. Football had been kind of tough on them (both the parents and the teeth).

I instantly fell in love with the 880-yard run. I was too slow to run the shorter events and was afraid of the longer ones. But twice around the track, just a half mile...that I could do.

Much to my surprise, I almost won my first race. One of my buddies nipped me right at the tape. I decided I wouldn't let that happen again.

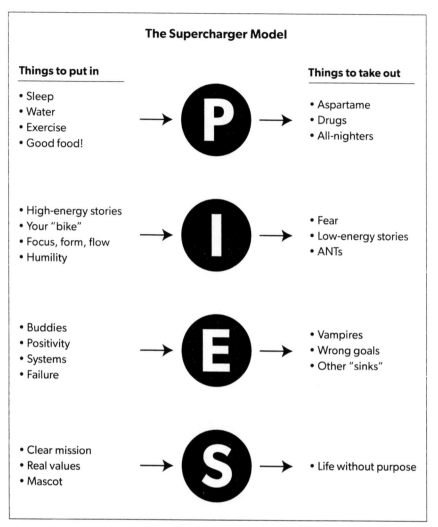

**The Supercharger Model**

| Things to put in | | Things to take out |
|---|---|---|

**P**

Things to put in:
- Sleep
- Water
- Exercise
- Good food!

Things to take out:
- Aspartame
- Drugs
- All-nighters

**I**

Things to put in:
- High-energy stories
- Your "bike"
- Focus, form, flow
- Humility

Things to take out:
- Fear
- Low-energy stories
- ANTs

**E**

Things to put in:
- Buddies
- Positivity
- Systems
- Failure

Things to take out:
- Vampires
- Wrong goals
- Other "sinks"

**S**

Things to put in:
- Clear mission
- Real values
- Mascot

Things to take out:
- Life without purpose

*Illustration #3: This Supercharger Model gives examples how you might refocus your life to boost energy and eliminate the "sinks" draining off your physical, intellectual, emotional and spiritual energy.*

And it pretty much didn't. After that, I adopted a simple strategy: just start running as fast as I could with 330 yards to go. Everybody else knew that was too early to start a sprint and so they let me go.

Of course, by the time I got to the finish line, rigor mortis had almost set in, but I was usually far enough ahead to hang on for the win. It was my first experience managing energy in competition.

In the fall of my sophomore year, I went out for cross-country, which didn't exactly break the hearts of the football coaches. Cross-country involved running 2.3 miles, a laughably short distance to runners these days, but a long, long run in 1964 for a school boy. (There was no girls cross-country team; the running authorities assumed it was too grueling for their frail hearts. Of course, today, my daughter Lee—and thousands of other women of all ages—routinely run marathons.)

Surprisingly, I liked cross-country. We trotted happily through the autumn woods and enjoyed much more visual variety than the 100 yards of gridiron offered. I discovered I was pretty good, too, even though it was much longer than a half mile. I even figured out how to turn right.

And so, at an early age, I learned one of the key secrets of physical energy: you have more than you thought you had.

*You can go a lot further than you think.*

## Intellectual Energy: The Power of Story

Thinking involves *Intellectual Energy*, often in the form of "stories" we tell ourselves—over and over again. Obviously, a story can add or subtract a lot of energy. Depending on the story you're telling yourself, you can do amazing things—good and bad—or nothing. Loehr's *Full Engagement* was so popular that he wrote a sequel, *The Power of Story*, that focused on just this point. So, here are some of my earliest "intellectual energy" stories....

At the tender age of 14, I decided to become a runner because of a one-sentence story the track coach told. I still remember it, even though it was a half century ago. We frosh sat in the audio-visual room for the "organizational" meeting for spring track. The coach said simply: "If you run for me for four years, I guarantee you'll get a college scholarship."

To a poor kid whose parents barely made it through high school, that sounded pretty good. (Clearly, I wasn't going to get recruited for football.) Like many intellectual energy stories, the coach's came true.

A small digression: it's said that the great chief Crazy Horse believed the story that his name's medicine was so powerful that he would never be wounded in battle. He never was. He was murdered on a peaceful visit to a fort. Of course, prior to that, he was very lucky; he was in many battles. *But think how you fight when you believe you cannot be wounded or killed.* Later in this book, we'll create your own energy "name" or mascot, hoping to harness this kind of power.

In the case of my energy story, I believed in my coach. And, in a strange way, I believed in the power of my shoes. It happened like this...

In my high school running career, I won several races, but in the *only one* that really mattered I finished second. I grew up in Rochester, NY, which has a permanent inferiority complex because it is in the same state with New York City.

So, when word leaked out that a running star from New York City was coming up to Rochester to challenge a local running phenom, there was a lot of buzz in the press, to say nothing of the high school running world. Much was made of this battle of the young speed merchants (neither of whom was me).

> **But think how you fight when you believe you cannot be wounded or killed.**

On the day of the big race, with hundreds of harriers fighting the Upstate New York chill, the local hero sped off with the Big Apple runner in hot pursuit. As usual, I was well back in the pack, enjoying a pair of new running shoes, which made me *feel* faster.

Like Crazy Horse pondering his invincibility, I told myself my new shoes actually *gave me an edge* over the guys with old shoes. I could beat them. Forgetting about the pain of the race, I gradually made my way toward the front of the pack. Suddenly, to my surprise, only the New Yorker, who had gone out too fast and was slowing dramatically, was between me and the local hero.

Thanks in part to my focus on my shoes, I beat the New Yorker and wound up with my picture in the paper with the local hero. Because I was thinking more about shoes than the pain, I somehow ran faster. I wasn't really conscious at the time of how much a different story made me a better runner.

The next day, the phone rang: "Did you ever think of going to Princeton?" the scout on the line asked. Well, no, I hadn't...until then. That was a whole different story.

Am I saying that thinking about shoes got me into Princeton? Even Nike wouldn't suggest that (especially since the shoes were Adidas). When you're talking energy, though, sometimes little things matter a lot. In so much of life, it's the extra little bit of effort that makes all the difference. In most races, all the runners have trained; the difference between the winners and the also-rans is often the slimmest of margins. Back in 1965, in an obscure cross-country race, a story made the difference.

Stories can give you extra intellectual juice…keep you in balance…and change your life.

## Emotional Energy: Vampires and Buddies

I've traveled the all over the country and spoken with many organizations, large and small, about managing personal energy. *Emotional Energy*, without question, gets the most discussion. It's because of the vampires.

We all know energy vampires. These soul-suckers can drain the energy out of a company, a team, a marriage, a career, a life. They are like little cancers, festering away, making everyone around them slower, weaker and more tired. They *love* to throw you off balance.

We all know energy buddies, too. With them, everything is easier: running, working, living…even odious tasks like filing documents and cleaning the garage.

When Roger Bannister set out to break the four-minute-mile barrier in the 1950s, many vampires thought that a person would die if they ran faster than four minutes. Bannister, who was a physician, knew better. He approached the problem scientifically—and with two energy buddies.

Realizing that the best chance of breaking the barrier was even, *balanced* pacing—four 60-second quarter-miles—he enlisted two other good runners to run with him. One to pace him for the first two laps, one for the critical third lap, and then he could "go for broke" alone in the final lap.[2]

> **Energy vampires can drain the energy out of a company, a team, a marriage, a career, a life.**

Today, sub-four-minute milers are commonplace. But in 1954, Bannister's feat was akin to climbing Everest for the first time. After he broke the record, running with "pacers" was declared illegal for a while—because the technique to keep the runner balanced was thought to be too easy. Such is the power of running with energy buddies. Today's record of 3:43.13 by Hicham el Garrouj was set with the help of pacing buddies.

Your buddies don't even have to run with you to be effective. Way back in the last century, I recall running one of the last races of my high school cross-country career: the 1966 Diocesan Championships. About a half mile from the finish, the little voice in my head said I was done. Not only was I really tired, but my feet hurt and I could barely breathe. Even worse, the trolls who had planned the course included a brutal up-hill finish—a real kick in the tail.

As I turned into that final climb, at the top of the hill stood my father, frantically waving big "come on" gestures. Somewhere, I mustered the horsepower to sprint up that hill. Past the finish line, I collapsed in the "chute." On all fours, I fought to stay conscious while my entire digestive system convulsed. Never, before or since, have I pushed that hard. But nobody caught me on that hill. Thanks, Dad.

Never underestimate the power of a good energy buddy.

## Spiritual Energy: The Power of Deep Inside

I have no idea what Martin Luther King's mile time was. He was a smoker, so it probably wasn't too good. Nor do I know how many push-ups Mother Theresa could do. And it's anybody's guess about how many pounds Mahatma Gandhi could dead lift (at 110 pounds, he would have been in the lowest weight class). But I do know that, because they could tap vast amounts of spiritual energy, all three changed the world.

*Spiritual Energy* is probably the least understood of all. For many, spiritual energy implies religion, but it doesn't have to. For me, the core of spiritual energy is *being who you are and doing what you do.* It's what you're looking for when you "find yourself." Later in the book, we'll discuss how discovering our own answers to life's basic questions can spark spiritual energy. It is the core energy that drives courage, passion and integrity. It tells us how to spend our time and our lives.

> **The core of spiritual energy is being who you are and doing what you do.**

Not long after I started running, my father gave me two key pieces of advice, each only a few words long, that have stood me in good stead for a lifetime of energy management. Both of them are about balance. The first admonishment was only two words: "Pace yourself." That one stretches nicely over physical, emotional and intellectual energy.

The second piece seemed tactical at first and then strategic and finally, spiritual.

"Run your own race," dad said simply. It means more than just running at your own pace; it means selecting the race you want to run. It reflects your calling, the core of spiritual energy. It's why I decided to write this book.

Spiritual energy differentiates us from animals. It is spiritual energy that makes us human.

## EnergyThink: How Do the PIES Energy "Fuel Tanks" Impact Your Life?

Back in 1965, a single good running performance was enough to attract Princeton's attention and start me on a whole new direction in life. But that little spark of intellectual and physical energy was only the *proximate* cause of what turned into a major life change. Go back far enough, like to the moment of conception, and a complex cocktail of energies created a mix of experiences that brought me to where I am today.

If you look back over your life, almost every change—the big ones and the little ones that often inevitably led to the larger ones—can be explained by energy.

What examples come to mind about:

⚡ Your physical energy? And how did they/do they change your life?

⚡ Your intellectual energy? And how did they/do they change your life?

⚡ Your emotional energy? And how did they/do they change your life?

⚡ Your spiritual energy? And how did they/do they change your life?

# 10

# Physical Sinks: Where the Juice Goes DOWN

**"I found out that it's not good to talk about my troubles. Eighty percent of the people who hear them don't care and the other twenty percent are glad you're having them." —Tommy LaSorda, LA Dodgers manager**

ENERGY IS LIKE A LOT OF OTHER THINGS: WHAT GOES *UP* USUALLY must come *DOWN*. Lots of things can slow you down: weight, old age, arthritis, creaky joints, not enough sleep, not enough good food, lack of exercise. I plead guilty to all of them.

It so happens that my favorite sport of long distance riding spotlights two of Americans' biggest energy drains or "sinks"[1]: eating (too much) and sleeping (not enough).

Because cyclists have to haul fat molecules up hills, the more competitive the cyclist, the more obsessed by weight he or she is. Pick almost any issue of *Bicycling Magazine* over the last three decades and the chances are excellent the cover will feature an article on losing weight. For example, the May 2014 issue trumpeted: "LEANER, FASTER, STRONGER: A Simple Plan to Get Fit and Lose Weight." In case you missed it, the October 2014 cover promised: "LEAN! STRONG! FAST! Your Simple Plan." The first story was about pedaling into old age ("The 50s & Beyond") and the second was based on the magazine's new book, *Bike Your Butt Off*.

Need I say more?

Some experts say that shaving just four pounds from bike and rider can be as effective as performance-enhancing drugs. Of course, the pros have already done everything they can do to lose weight (it's why some of them look like concentration camp victims)...so drugs loom as a ready alternative.

When I raced Paris-Brest-Paris the first time in 2007, I skinnied down to 168 pounds—my lowest since high school. PBP is moderately hilly and I noticed the difference it made compared to my usual 175 pounds. I was faster and my tender knees complained a lot less.

So, why don't we all just go out and lose a bunch of weight? It's the very question I ask myself every time I'm sitting in the middle seat on an airplane between two 250-pounders.

At this point, we will pause while you recall:

⚡ The calorie-counting app on your smart phone;

⚡ Articles on losing weight your friends sent you;

⚡ The time you tried going gluten-free;

⚡ That vegetarian diet you promised yourself last New Year's;

⚡ The dirty looks the Food Nazis give you in the supermarket.

## The Cream Puff Diet

Now, take a deep breath: are you ready for "Greg's 20 Tips to a Thinner You"? Well, you can stop holding your breath. This is no diet book. No tips. No magic diets. I probably eat the same junk you do.

> **Go to Italy. Do you see a lot of fat Italians?**

Of course, food has a big impact on energy. Of course, it's better to lose those extra inches. Duh. You need a book to tell you that? I don't think so.

These days, food allergies are big. I go to the doctor and he says: "You're allergic to wheat, eggs, and sugar."

"So my mother's cream puffs are killing me?" I ask.

"That's right," he says.

"You gotta die of something," I say. You see, I grew up Italian. And I always believed that my mom makes cream puffs to die for. Now I know it's true.

So, take "Noni" Conderacci's advice:

You tired? *Mangia!*
You sick? *Mangia!*
You feeling a little sad? *Mangia!*
You lose your girlfriend? *Mangia!*
You lose your car keys? *Mangia!*
You want to win that race? *Mangia!*

Don't knock eating, I say. It works. My mother is 92. She eats her cream puffs. Go to Italy. Do you see a lot of fat Italians? Nope. They eat their mothers' cream puffs, too.

## Death to Diet Coke

But there is one thing I will not put in my mouth: Aspartame, the drug of choice for everybody who *thinks* they are losing weight by eating and drinking it. Make no mistake: I *heart* Diet Coke. I used to drink a lot of it.

I did, that is, until one morning when I suddenly developed a crippling pain in my left leg. The discomfort came on suddenly and gradually built over about three hours. My left leg felt like it had just run a marathon, but my right leg felt fine. And I hadn't done any strenuous exercise.

Just as I thought I had thrown a clot and needed to go to the hospital, the pain suddenly vanished. Then, of course, I *knew* I had to go to the hospital.

"What's you're problem, sir?" the emergency room receptionist asked.

"I am completely pain free," I said.

"That's not a symptom, sir," she said.

"It is for me," I said. After I explained, the hospital did a complete, exhaustive examination. They could find nothing wrong with me.

A week later, it happened again. Severe pain that started suddenly and disappeared five hours later just as quickly.

I visited my internist at the prestigious Johns Hopkins Hospital. A full battery of tests were all negative.

Then I had breakfast with a friend, Christina Chambreau, who is (no kidding) a homeopathic veterinarian. When I described the symptoms, she didn't hesitate for a minute: "It's Aspartame poisoning. Do you drink Diet Coke?"

> There is one thing I will not put in my mouth: Aspartame.

Then, I remembered another friend whose seizures were caused by Diet Coke. (The docs thought he had MS.) And another friend who thought her memory loss was caused by early Alzheimer's. (Again, stopping the diet drinks solved her problem.) I cut all the Aspartame from my diet and the symptoms never returned. You think I'm kidding? Go ahead and Google "Aspartame side effects."[2]

So, I ask you: Do you see a lot of fat people around you? What are they drinking? Do they look good to you? Do you sense a little unbalance here? Trade the diet drinks for the cream puffs.

## Which High Energy Drink Has Zero Calories?

You could try water. Water is Mother Nature's best energy drink. No calories, but it actually boosts performance. That's because most of the time most of us are dehydrated. Dry people don't do as well as wet people.

Think about it: we're 57% water.[3] In a fully hydrated state, there is more blood to carry more energy around our bodies. In bicycle racing, water is key and dehydration can literally mean death.

In major stage races like the Tour de France, cyclists are often rehydrated intravenously during the evenings between stages. That's because it's often hard to replace the fluids lost during a long day of racing.

Usually, though, most of us can hydrate the old fashioned way...by drinking. In ultra-distance events, I often carry two bottles of water, laced with Hammer Perpetuum and HEED, on my bike and a hydropack on my back full of plain water. Essentially, I'm lugging a gallon of water—more than eight pounds in a weight-conscious sport.

I gladly pay the weight penalty because I've ridden with dehydrated riders (and been one myself many

> **Water is Mother Nature's best energy drink.**

times). Severe dehydration is not a pretty sight. I once raced with a rider who could not drink enough to replace the water he lost in sweat.

He was fine in events of less than 300 kilometers (about 190 miles), but faced a crisis when racing at 400 kilometers (250 miles) or more. For him, dehydration was like letting the air out of his tires. His energy would fade suddenly. By then, it was too late. He would limp along weakly for a while, clearly in trouble. In a couple races, I fell back to ride with him because I was concerned he would collapse. At one point, he couldn't drink; everything that went down came right back up. That's 911 time.

Most of us are dehydrated because we rely on thirst to tell us when to drink. By the time we are thirsty, we're already long gone. When I'm riding, I drink at least a full 24-ounce bottle every hour, more if it's really hot. I never, ever want to be thirsty. Too dangerous.

I practice building up my toleration for heat and fluid loss by frequent trips to my favorite yoga studio, Baltimore Hot Yoga & Wellness. For more than a decade, the owner, Debbie Vojik, has been twisting me into pretzel shapes in 105-degree heat. Not only does it help heal my sore riding muscles, but I've gotten used to sweating quarts in a matter of minutes. And, it literally improves my balance.

> **There's no delicate way to say this: If you look down into the potty and you see yellow, you're dehydrated.**

How can you tell if you're properly hydrated? Clear urine. There's no delicate way to say this: If you look down into the potty and you see yellow, you're dehydrated.

Another bonus is that water fills you up, you feel less hungry, and so you're less tempted to eat that snack that you shouldn't...

The great irony is that we Americans are relatively water rich. Usually, we can drink all we want, often essentially for free, from a nearby tap or fountain. My first experience with the global challenge of finding clean, fresh water came in 2006 on Mount Kilimanjaro. Climbing to the "Roof of Africa" means that you must gather water in what is essentially an arctic desert.

Every night, you draw water from the streams trickling from the melting glaciers on the mountain and laboriously pump it through filters to ensure that it is potable. It's a lot of work. And that's nothing compared to what most of the world's population has to do to get water.

Once you've had to work hard for the water to stay alive, you realize what a gift it is to get it so easily.

## EnergyThink: What Could You Do... Free and Easy?

Many of the biggest physical energy boosters are free. The secret is looking for "adjacent possibilities." Adjacent possibilities are those activities that don't demand a lot of extra energy, money, time or thought. They're pretty easy to identify. We used to call them "next steps." In my energy seminars, I ask participants what they could do next... without losing their balance.

Running a marathon if you've only run a couple miles in your life is not a next step. Here are some simple examples:

⚡ Could you drink a little extra water?

⚡ Could you sleep a half hour longer?

⚡ Could you go for a short walk a few times a week?

⚡ Could you substitute unsweetened ice tea for soft drinks?

⚡ What else could be a "next step" for you?

# 11

# Sleep! Sleep! Sleep!

— — — — — — — — — — — — — —

**"When I woke up this morning, my girlfriend asked me, 'Did you sleep good?' I said, 'No, I made a few mistakes.'" —Comedian Steven Wright**

— — — — — — — — — — — — — —

HERE'S ANOTHER THING YOU COULD TRY: SLEEP. STUDIES SHOW THE average American sleeps about six hours a night. A hundred years ago, before they invented Monday Night Football, the average American slept more than eight. Indeed, the Gallup Poll found that 40% of Americans get less than seven hours today—more than an hour less than the 7.9 hours average in 1942 when it first polled on the question.[1]

For the past 50,000 years, people slept eight to ten. Don't ask me how they kept up with Facebook.

So, here we are, pushing back against evolution. Do you think that the "sleep imbalance" might explain why we:

⚡ Feel so tired?

⚡ Are so impatient and cranky?

⚡ Are depressed?

⚡ Look so old?

⚡ Get sick so much?

⚡ Can't concentrate?

⚡ Take more time to get even simple things done?

## Ride... or Sleep?

Unlike those sissies in the Tour de France, we ultra-long-distance cyclists don't get an official "time out" every night. In every event, we have the happy option of riding from start to finish without sleeping. That's usually very possible in events of 250 miles or less.

But when the distances increase to 400 miles, 600 miles, 750 miles or even 1,000 miles, sleep becomes a major strategic factor. Complicating matters is the fact that many events begin in the evening.

When I raced the 1001 Miglia in Italy in 2012, the 1,001-mile competition began at 9 pm and we rode straight through the night across the great plains southeast of Milan. When the sun came up, the road tipped up into the mountains.

The ride organizers seemed to take to heart God's promise in Isaiah: "I will make you ride on the heights of the earth." It's hard to say which is more fun: climbing when you've had no sleep or descending when you've had no sleep. On the way up, you're going too slow and on the way down... well, miss a hairpin turn and they'll never find you again.

> **The roads feature what my Italian guide friend Angelo calls "hair-spin" turns.**

Toward the end of the race, the course dips into the Cinque Terra, the beautiful but rugged coastline in the northwestern part of the "Boot." Here the road drops precipitously into one quaint little town on the Ligurian Sea only to soar again before reaching another. The roads feature what my Italian guide friend Angelo calls "hair-spin" turns. I like the term much better than "hairpin," since the prospect of spinning out on one of these turns makes my hair stand on end. It's the ultimate loss of balance.

Race or no race, I desperately needed sleep before tackling the Cinque Terra. But no hotelier would take me. Imagine a dirty, foul-smelling cyclist appearing in your lobby in the middle of the night, speaking bad broken Italian and begging for a room for four hours.

"Non mi dispiace," the clerks all said, "No, I am sorry." There were no vacancies. Finally, I woke up a nice guy who ran a quaint bed and breakfast. He was a little miffed that I would not be staying for breakfast, but he gave me a bed... and saved me from falling asleep and losing my balance on a "hair-spin." [2]

## Paris–Brest–PariZZZZZZ

In the famous Paris–Brest–Paris race, the Olympics of Randonneuring, 5,000 of the world's best gather every four years. It is cycling's oldest race, dating back to 1891. Traditionally, the race starts in the evening. There is also an option to start the following morning. If you choose the former start, you get 90 hours to finish; the latter, only 84. It's a big issue, because the racers have spent thousands of dollars and hundreds of hours preparing for it. To race, and not to finish, is hard.

So the time managers, a group that includes most of the riders, choose the "safer" evening start. Both times I raced PBP, I chose the morning start. During the race, I also actually slept in a real bed in a hotel, considered a true luxury by many riders who sleep on the road (literally), on park benches, in doorways and on the floors of school gyms.

I believe it is better to sleep and ride faster than not to sleep and ride slower. It's also a lot more pleasant.

> **I believe it is better to sleep and ride faster than not to sleep and ride slower. It's also a lot more pleasant.**

I've transferred that philosophy into my life, too. I strive for at least seven hours sleep a night, even if it means shutting down the computer before all the email is answered. Like most of us, I thought I was a "night person" until I discovered that, rather than struggle through a problem late at night, I could dispatch it promptly in the morning.

In a fascinating TED video, brain researcher Jeff Iliff points out something we all know: when we sleep, it clears our mind; when we don't, it leaves our minds "murky." He found that sleep might actually allow the brain to rid itself of harmful waste products and take on nutrients. No small matter, since the brain routinely consumes about 20% of our caloric intake and generates a lot of waste (some of which takes the form of bad knock-knock jokes). Failing to get enough good quality sleep makes the brain fall behind on its "housekeeping" and may even contribute to Alzheimer's disease, he says.[3]

Although the literature on sleep is vast, we still don't know for sure why we do it. We just know we need it. Without it, we don't have the energy we need. Without it, everything... takes... more... time.

## A Presidential Siesta Defeats the "Nap Zone"

Early in his career, one of my grad school profs had worked for President Lyndon Johnson. The professor said Johnson was in the habit of rising very early in the morning, working until mid-afternoon and then taking an extended nap. After the nap, he would work several more hours, essentially working two days in one.

Research on pilots has shown that a mid-afternoon nap improves performance 34%.[4] Perhaps there is a reason many cultures knock off in the middle of the afternoon, during the dreaded "Nap Zone" of 2 to 4 pm. Certainly, 3 pm is usually *not* a good time to have a meeting.

Similarly, there is a parallel "Sleep Zone" around 2 to 4 AM. (Even the Bible talks about how difficult the "watch before dawn" is. It's during the fourth watch, which begins at 3 a.m. that Jesus walks on the water toward the storm-tossed disciples in the small boat.) Take it from a rider who has been on the road during those hours. Even on races of hundreds of miles over several days, I try to be asleep during those hours. If you're driving, this is a dangerous time… especially if the bars close at 2.

## The Curse of the French All-Nighter

Nowadays, if I'm pulling an all-nighter, I'm doing a "fleche" (pronounced "flesh," as in "I hate this frigging fleche"). French riders invented this event to torture otherwise sane riders who sleep. The event requires a team of four or five riders to ride at least 240 miles in 24 hours, give or take 10 minutes. To make it interesting, riders cannot stop at any one point for more than two hours. In other words, no sleep.

Of course, there usually is no shortage of drama as a group of riders, operating on scant sleep, struggle to get along. The rules don't say it specifically, but it's illegal to kill any of the riders, an idea that has occurred to many a racer. They do allow as many as two not to finish before the team is disqualified.

**One year, we disposed of a body at a police station.**

One year, we disposed of a body at a police station. No kidding. By tradition, fleches take place in the wet and cold early spring, ideal hypothermia weather. On my first fleche, when one of our teammates become so hypothermic he couldn't go on, we stopped at the station, where they threw him in a hot shower, wrapped him in a blanket and put him in a cell. We pressed on. *Oui!*

Everyone recalls the all-nighters in their lives: cramming for a test in college, jamming to get a project done on time, struggling to get everything done before a wedding or a vacation. If you think back upon them, two facts emerge: afterwards, you looked terrible and you didn't remember much. And maybe you gained weight.

There's science behind all three findings.

First, lack of sleep seems to prevent the mental "trigger" that releases human growth hormone from firing. So the natural process of repair that occurs during sleep never happens. If you cheat on sleep repeatedly, there is evidence you will age faster and be weaker.

Second, apparently, the brain needs the sleep period to imprint the memories accumulated over the course of the day. Experiments with rats demonstrate that, if a rat's sleep is shortened or disrupted, it has to re-learn the same maze it solved the day before.[5] Maybe that explains why we no longer remember anything we learned while cramming for exams.

> **Sumo wrestlers, who are striving for maximum weight gain, eat once a day—right before bed.**

Third, if we are awake much past sundown, the ancient DNA-based wiring in our brains registers danger, even if there is none. It's as if a little voice in our heads is saying, "Wow! It's dark and you're not asleep. The village must be on fire. Maybe there's a bear in the cave. You need energy. You'd better eat."

Anyone who has experienced the "munchies" at 9 or 10 pm (don't we all?) can identify with this. Of course, it's the absolute worst time to eat if you want to lose weight. Sumo wrestlers, who are striving for maximum weight gain, eat once a day—right before bed.

## Sleeping Through Your Next Diet

In an article in the National Institute of Health's *Archives of Disease in Childhood*, S. Taheri contends that "On the basis of both population studies and laboratory studies on partial sleep restriction, there is increasing evidence that short sleep duration results in metabolic changes that may contribute to the development of obesity, insulin resistance, diabetes and cardiovascular disease."

Why? Because, Taheri argues, citing 13 different studies, "Short sleep duration can affect both energy intake and energy expenditure. It results in tiredness that may hamper physical activity, and alters metabolic hormones to increase appetite and affect food selection. Additionally, extra time awake provides increased opportunity for food intake."[6]

Yes, boys and girls, the longer you are awake, the more time you have to eat. Think about it; it's logical.

So in the end, perhaps there is a link between losing sleep and gaining weight, two of America's biggest physical challenges.

## EnergyThink: Could You Sleep Just a Little More?

Shakespeare's Macbeth morns his loss of:

> "….The innocent sleep,
> Sleep that knits up the raveled sleeve of care,
> The death of each day's life, sore labor's bath,
> Balm of hurt minds, great nature's second course,
> Chief nourisher in life's feast." (Act 2, Scene 2)

You're probably *not* going to go from sleeping only six hours a night to sleeping eight or ten and enjoying your "chief nourisher." After all, you've designed your life around six hours. BUT…

⚡ If you're like many people, though, the last half hour of being awake in the evening isn't very productive. Could you go to bed a bit earlier? You're not giving up much.

⚡ If you can't get seven, eight or more hours every night, could you at least get in the habit of a few extra hours on certain days of the week, like Sunday and Wednesday nights? You'd start the week fresher and get over the "hump" easier.

⚡ Many folks become fans of more sleep when they discover that they are far more efficient (and life is more pleasant) when they're well rested. Will you give it a try?

**PART FOUR**

# Understanding
# Intellectual Energy

# 12

# Intellectual Energy: Your Brain on a Bike

- - - - - - - - - - - - - - - -

**" 'Tis nothing good or bad, but thinking makes it so." —William Shakespeare**

- - - - - - - - - - - - - -

CONSIDER THE LOWLY BICYCLE, PERHAPS ONE OF THE MOST EFFICIENT machines ever built:

⚡ By riding a device that weighs a tenth of your weight, you can go ten times as far with the same amount of energy.

⚡ Marathoners are exhausted after their event, but many folks can ride 26.2 miles—faster than world class runners—without even getting out of breath.

⚡ Rides of a hundred miles a day on a bicycle are not only possible, but common.[1]

⚡ Bicycling is about leverage—using your energy far more efficiently.

Wouldn't it be nice if you could leverage your brain power the way a bike leverages your muscle power?

You certainly would be way ahead of where you are now. Think about it: in our modern society, mental energy is highly prized and often lavishly rewarded. Mental energy organizes our lives. It solves problems large and small. It invents technology from iPhones to ATMs. It creates great paintings and award-winning performances. It negotiates billion-dollar deals. It keeps us in balance.

It even helps quarterbacks spot open receivers. In fact, the National Football League has even developed a test, the Wonderlic, to measure it.

It's 50 questions long and every college senior who wants to play in the NFL takes the test. A great score would be getting half the questions right.

## Your Own Wonderlic

Care to give it a try? I'm borrowing some typical questions from *Thinking Fast and Slow*, Noble Laureate Daniel Kahneman's brilliant brain book. Just read the five questions below quickly and scribble down your answers. No peeking at the answers just below the questions. Do all the work in your head: no calculators; don't even write out the math on a piece of paper.

Here goes:

1. $17 \times 24 =$ _____

2. A bat and a ball cost $1.10. The bat costs one dollar more than the ball. How much does the ball cost? _____

3. If it takes 5 machines 5 minutes to make 5 widgets, how long would it take 100 machines to make 100 widgets? _____

4. In a lake, there is a patch of lily pads. Every day, the patch doubles in size. If it takes 48 days for the patch to cover the entire lake, how long would it take for the patch to cover half the lake? _____

5. How many animals of each species did Moses have on the Ark? _____

If you're anything like me and many of the people in my energy management classes, you immediately gave up on the very first question. A little voice in your head was complaining:

> **WHAT? Multiply two two-digit numbers in my head? You can't be serious.**

*WHAT? Multiply two two-digit numbers in my head? You can't be serious. Don't you see there's a SEVEN in there? Nobody multiplies by seven any more, much less 17. If God wanted us to multiply by 17, He wouldn't have given us calculators.*

It is, of course, very possible to do the calculation in your head. In 2007, Alexis Lemaire found the 13th root of a 200 digit number in his head.[2] Here's the number:

83689566882369569398373286622256452247267804664938366774
97357558157303507570408962528802385783156837680293493820l
05634336385559593151445041514949070941909770444930566026
84027718696241556880826486409933

The answer, as we all know, is 2391481494636373. Right? It took him 70 seconds to do the calculation. That's probably faster than it took you to do my quickie version of the Wonderlic. Here are those answers:

1. 17 x 24 = 408

2. Ball costs 5 cents

3. 5 minutes to make 100 widgets

4. 47 days to cover half the lake

5. Zero; Moses didn't have an ark; Noah did.

I'll bet you missed that last one.

## It's a L.I.E.!

How did you do? Whether you aced the test or not is unimportant. What is important is that you probably experienced low intellectual energy. Here are some other symptoms of L.I.E. Do you...

- ⚡ Become sidetracked easily?
- ⚡ Lose concentration?
- ⚡ Misplace things?
- ⚡ Experience failures of short-term memory?
- ⚡ Feel you are not making progress?
- ⚡ See declining analytical skills?
- ⚡ Have difficulty organizing your work schedule?
- ⚡ Procrastinate?[3]

I plead guilty on all counts. No wonder Kahneman refers to the part of our brain that does the heavy intellectual lifting as "The Lazy Controller."

Although we have this super computer between our ears, using even a bit of its incredible potential is a lot of work.

Kahneman has a formal name for The Lazy Controller: "System Two." This is the part of our brain that is "smarter"—or at least it *thinks* it is. I like to think of System Two like Han Solo, the swashbuckling but flawed hero of the old *Star Wars* movies. By contrast, the more emotional, "automatic" part of our brains is dubbed "System One" by Kahneman. That reminds me of Solo's big furry sidekick, Chewbacca the Wookie (strong, but not too smart). We'll be spending more time with him later in the book.

## EnergyThink: Mental Heavy Lifting

⚡ Are your "low energy" symptoms getting more frequent? Why? (Don't say: "Because I'm getting older"!!!)

⚡ What could you do to counteract those trends?

⚡ Are you "giving up too soon" when confronted with an intellectual energy challenge? Try shifting the activity that's taxing you to a more high-energy time—perhaps earlier in the morning, if you're stronger then.

⚡ Have you been doing these "EnergyThink" exercises to this point? No? Now you know why: Low Intellectual Energy!

# 13

# Shift Happens:
# Finding Your "Miracle Bike"

— — — — — — — — — — — — — — —

**"Life is like a ten speed bicycle. Most of us have
gears we never use." —Charles M. Schulz**

— — — — — — — — — — — — — — —

INTELLECTUAL ENERGY ISN'T ONLY AN IMPORTANT PART OF LIFE; LIKE
balance, it's a big part of cycling, too. To illustrate, I will share the Story
of the Two Tooth Miracles.

"I've never seen anyone heal so fast," the oral surgeon said, peering into
my mouth, snapping pictures of my 20-year-old gums minus the wisdom
teeth he had recently crow-barred out of my jaw. The dentist was a happy
man. So proud of his handiwork, he announced he would be using my case
in his dental school lectures.

*Flash. Flash. Flash.* The good doctor clicked away as I closed my eyes
to keep from going blind from point-blank photography. My mouth was
going to be famous.

But he didn't know half the story.

*It was the bicycle.* The bicycle had healed, in record time, the gaps he
had left in my mouth. The dentist had ordered me not to ride my new
bike until my mouth healed. So I was motivated to heal. Because of the
bike, I had shifted from slow healing to fast healing. It was 1969, and my
long love affair with my machine was young, so I didn't understand the
significance of the event.

It was Tooth Miracle Number One.

## Tooth Miracle #2
Tooth Miracle Number Two was a bit more dramatic.

"Did you have front teeth when you started your ride?" the emergency medical technician asked, as I slowly regained consciousness in the ambulance. It was 2010. After more than four decades of riding, I had a better grasp on my miraculous machine. Except that my 20-speed friend and I had just shared a near-death experience: losing our balance on a steel bridge.

A passing pickup driver had scraped the two of us, both broken, off the span. He stuffed us in his truck and whisked us off to the local volunteer fire department. The vols left the bike behind, jammed me into the ambulance and sped away to the hospital. Pretty soon, my gap-toothed mouth was going to be photographed again.

Between the Tooth Miracles, I have experienced many more, thanks to my trusty two-wheeled steeds. They have helped heal many wounds—physical and otherwise. They have blessed me with almost boundless energy. They have brought back balance when I have faltered. They have stopped the march of time in its tracks. They have accelerated my career. They have supplied self-confidence when I needed it most. They have enriched my life with adventure. They help make me happy.

They taught me to shift.

## It's All About Good Shift

For the beginner cyclist, one of the most daunting challenges is mastering gear shifting. Unlike a car, which automatically shifts itself or has a few "manual" gears, a bike can have as many as 33. There can be up to 11 different cogs in the back around the rear wheels and up to three chain rings in the front where the pedals are. The "front" is shifted by the left hand; the "rear" is shifted by the right.

Confused yet? Does this sound like another Wonderlic? It gets worse.

The gearing "overlaps." So, for a rider to move to progressively higher or lower gears he or she must often be shifting with both hands simultaneously. It can be like playing one of those electric guitars with two necks. (Well, not really, but I'm hunting for a metaphor here; be patient with me, musicians.) Figuring all this out can be so mentally complex that many new riders will ride the bicycle in only one or two gears—even though that is *much more* physically taxing.

TMI, right? Yeah, too much information. In fact, you're probably getting ready to drop this book now. Yep. That's exactly the feeling new riders get confronting all those bewildering gears. Bike shop owners will tell you that folks return bikes with oil tracks on only one or two of those gears. Some people just don't like shifting.[1]

Why all the gears? Because good riders *want* to shift. Subtle differences in speed, terrain, wind or competitive situations demand almost constant gear changes. Gears make riding easier and more efficient.... and more balanced.

Like this...

> **Some people just don't like shifting.**

*Flying along in a fast pack, sheltering from the wind behind a nice big guy, everything is dandy until ... three riders launch off the front of the group. Two clicks of the right gear lever gives me the extra speed to catch them, until... the road tips sharply upward and then a click of the left lever dumps me into a significantly lower gear, but... it will be too low and I'll lose momentum unless I simultaneously add two more clicks of the right. Then everybody slows toward the top and I back off three clicks on the right, until... we go over the top and then I shift up one click left and six on the right together...*

Whew! See what I mean?

Sometimes, shifting seems like a lot of trouble. So we stay in the same job and just work harder. We keep having the same difficult relationships because we're afraid to shift the conversation. We delay insulating the house, even though it would be cheaper and more comfortable to do so. We stick with the same frameworks that leave us feeling trapped and sapped, unbalanced prisoners of the world around us.

Yet we can all change gears. Right there, right at your fingertips on your (real or imaginary) bike, is a little gear shift lever. Push it, and you can go uphill easier. Push it again, and you can go downhill faster. Push it to get through headwinds. Push it when you get tired. Push it when you need to keep on going.

You wouldn't play a round of golf with just one club. You wouldn't go hiking in dress shoes. In life and in cycling, you have to change. It's easier to push the shift lever than to struggle against the wind.

Why don't we do it?

## Leverage: Finding Your Bicycle

This is *not* an advertisement for bicycles. Bicycles are inert devices of metal, carbon, and rubber. They know nothing; on their own, they do nothing. Former national champion John Howard said, "The bicycle is a curious vehicle. Its passenger is its engine." We are our lives' own engine. We can change. We can find *our own bicycles*. It's not about picking one out in the local bike shop. It's not even about the two-wheeled, pedaled variety.

*It's about choosing the things and the thinking that give you energy and using them to change your life*. It's not the "thing" itself. It's what the "thing" and you do together. Like Picasso and paint. Like Yo-Yo Ma and the cello. Like Mickey Mantle and the bat. Just like on a bicycle, you and your thing are in balance. Find a "bicycle"…whatever that is…for you. Get *UP* on your bike!

## EnergyThink: What's YOUR Bicycle?

When you look for your "bicycle," look for leverage. Like a microscope magnifying your vision, bicycles multiply your energy—in every sense of the word. Really, you can *live* on a bicycle for days, traveling hundreds of miles. I've done it.

Early in the history of this marvelous machine, its efficiency captured the imagination of its devotees. It still does. The bicycle tells its owner: *you can go farther than you think*. It is an incredibly powerful message. It's an energy message that goes well beyond the physical. Those of us who listen to it are unceasingly surprised by what a bicycle's puny human engine can do…even when we're not riding.

In my energy seminars, I like using the bicycle metaphor because almost everyone has ridden a bike. Unlike sophisticated technical equipment, musical instruments or fancy sports gear, bicycles are not beyond our imagination. So, use your imagination:

⚡ What is *your* bicycle? What activity or tool is a "force multiplier" for your energy?

⚡ You can use your intellectual energy to give you more of all kinds of other energy. Energy feeds on itself. Think about things or activities or places that give you more physical, intellectual, emotional and spiritual energy. The beach? The shopping mall? The synagogue? The back porch? The canoe? The skis? The car?

⚡ Think about things you *love* to do. Is there a symbol or a image that stays with you…that gives you "juice" every time you see it?

# 14

# Plunging into Intellectual Energy Sinks

—  —  —  —  —  —  —  —  —  —  —  —  —

**"Life is hard. It's harder if you're stupid." —John Wayne**

—  —  —  —  —  —  —  —  —  —  —  —  —

NOT ONLY IS USING INTELLECTUAL ENERGY HARD WORK, THERE ARE plenty of "sinks" that will effectively drain away what little we can marshal. Here are some of my favorites, based on the book *Strengthening Your Work Skills*.

**Avoiding negative outcomes versus seeking positive results.** How do you avoid being in an automobile accident? Simple: never ride in a car. While most of us would dismiss that out of hand, many of us are reluctant to take even modest risks because we fear the outcomes. As a teacher, I'll frequently ask a question with an easy, even obvious answer, yet few students will volunteer a reply. When everyone knows the answer, but no one will raise his or her hand, I know the "avoiding negative outcomes" sink is sucking energy out of the class.

As an employer, I often noticed employees who worked hard to make their jobs smaller. Somehow, they got the idea that the less they did, the less risk they took. What were they thinking? Did they read someplace in the employee handbook that "Nobody ever got fired for doing nothing"? In my energy seminars, I always see heads nodding in recognition of this phenomenon.

**The Universal Donor.** The expression originates in health care where those with type O negative blood were thought to be able to donate to everyone. In energy, "universal donors" are those who can't say "no." Anyone can take their energy. And, invariably, everybody does, leaving little behind. In his very funny 2013 TED talk,[1] David Grady calls our tendency to automatically accept computer-based meeting invitations "The Mindless Accept

Syndrome" or MAS. His solution: "No MAS"—the Spanish expression for "I've had enough!"

**Unclear or conflicting objectives.** "When you don't know where you're going, any road will take you there" goes the old saw. If the goal is vague, so is the performance. Conflicting objectives create "spin." Spin is that unsettled state that has you starting many projects and finishing none. When you do finish a task in a spin situation, it often is an easy, low-priority one. The truly important objectives often will get "a lick and a promise." We *think* we are multitasking, that wonderful 21st Century skill. But in fact we are concentrating on nothing long enough to get it done properly and efficiently. (See spin example below under "Interruptions.")

**Intermittents.** Would you rather have a car that started in the morning *sometimes*—or never? I'd much prefer the latter, because you can fix a car that doesn't start. And you can count on it not starting. Not knowing whether...

⚡ She will show up or...

⚡ He will be in a good mood or...

⚡ A trick will work or...

⚡ The report will be on time... is really challenging.

> **Spin is that unsettled state that has you starting many projects and finishing none.**

**Interruptions**. Once upon a time, this used to mean an untimely visit from a co-worker in a neighboring office or an unnecessary phone call from home. Of course, those are still around. The recent trend to "open offices," where every conversation is a public conversation, makes those interruptions much more common.

Modern technology has raised interruptions to a whole new level. Email, texting, social media like Facebook and Twitter, and the ever-present temptations of the internet have spawned a brand new syndrome: Attention Deficit Trait.

Edward Hallowell, author of *Driven to Distraction,* says that ADT mimics Attention Deficit Disorder in people who never had that condition. Technology has showered them with a "cacophony of mental noise," destroying their ability to control impulses. They are constantly checking their smart phones and computers, while their productivity crashes and mistakes soar. Like this:

*Hmmm. Perhaps I should check email to see if the boss changed his mind again…. Nope, but there's a great sale on Amazon. Maybe I should check their website. Wow! 50% off! I should text Bill and Mary to let them know…. Didn't Mary mention on her Facebook page that she got 40% off last week? Yep, there's her posting… Oh, and now she's suggesting a great YouTube video. I'll just click on that link and watch for a minute…. When am I supposed to pick up the kids? Oh, look, three more Evites on the calendar for this weekend….Might not have time to catch that new flick, but it looks just great. You know, Joe would love it. Better send him the link to the trailer. Checking email again… Look at that stupid comment on Huffington Post…what's THAT all about? Interesting… and look at the picture of Angelina Jolie…. Whoa, breaking news from The New York Times! Hope it's not serious…OMG…have to pick up milk and eggs on the way home…. No time to cook tonight. Let's see where Yelp suggests I should grab dinner…*

## EnergyThink: Don't Be an Energy Turtle

On some bike rides, turtle rescue emerges as a major work of mercy. Once, on a 30 mile ride, I "saved" a half dozen, stopping to lift the slow-moving little buggers off the highway and safely onto the other side of the road. I'm sure they were terrified and annoyed when I picked them up.

Don't you know people like that? They feel very secure in their own little "shells" of stories. Their world looks just fine to them: the road is flat, smooth, warm and easy to crawl over. They see no reason to go any faster or to go another way. This is the way all the other turtles do it.

Don't be an Energy Turtle:

⚡ How are you getting across the highway?

⚡ Run down the above list of intellectual energy sinks. Which ones are your biggest issues? Can you think of others?

⚡ Is your technology leveraging your intellectual energy… or hobbling it?

⚡ Can you feel the effects of Attention Deficit Trait?

⚡ What might you do to reduce its impact?

# 15

# What's Your Story?

---

---

INTELLECTUAL ENERGY IS STORY-DRIVEN; IT'S ABOUT YOUR IDEAS AND beliefs.

Having twice crossed this vast United States on a bicycle, I can attest to the phenomenon of The Great Plains: the road goes on forever in a straight line between nothing but wheat, corn and soybeans. It's hot. A rider can think:

> **Story #1:** *"What am doing here? What was I thinking when I signed up for this? This ride is so mind-numbingly boring that I will soon be crazy if I am not already. And this saddle is killing me. And the knees aren't too happy, either. They're getting worse every day. I don't know if I can make it."*

OR...

> **Story #2:** *"What a great way to see the country! I had no idea how big and rich it is. The weather is wonderful; sunny with no rain. The temperature makes it much easier on these sore muscles. Look how far I've come; even if I don't make it, this will be a real accomplishment."*

Both stories are true. One gives energy and one takes it away. I don't have to lie to myself or even hope for anything. All I have to do is select which story I'm going to run in a continuous loop in my brain.

## A Kilimanjaro Mountain Sickness "Diagnosis"

This is a story about how stories can help you climb to the top...or stop you in your tracks.

I climbed Mt. Kilimanjaro in 2006. Ernest Hemmingway begins his famous short story, "The Snows of Kilimanjaro," with this epigraph:

> Kilimanjaro is a snow-covered mountain, 19,710 feet high, and is said to be the highest mountain in Africa. Its western summit is called the Masai "Ngaje Ngai," the House of God. Close to the western summit there is the dried and frozen carcass of a leopard. No one has explained what the leopard was seeking at that altitude.

Having been on the mountain, I share a special appreciation for the leopard mystery. There is nothing attractive about the moonscape summit and the oxygen-stingy air that would draw any sane animal, including humans, to the top.

"The Snows of Kilimanjaro" is fiction. One of the *true* stories they tell you before you go up is that Mountain Sickness can kill you. Water in your lungs (high altitude pulmonary edema or HAPE) or in your brain (high altitude cerebral edema or HACE)

> **It was c-c-c-cold. Real leopard-freezing weather.**

is not good. The "Roof of Africa" is about mile higher than anything in the Lower 48 States, so there is really no way for homebound Americans to know whether they will suffer from Mountain Sickness until they get to the mountain. Although it's rare, every year climbers die from HACE or HAPE there.

And that's where my story begins. I was fortunate enough to be climbing with a couple of medical doctors, both outstanding in their fields and both great guys and solid climbers. On summit day, we set out together from our base camp at 15,000 feet in the wee hours of the morning, hoping to reach the peak shortly after dawn.

It was c-c-c-cold. Real leopard-freezing weather. I didn't need to look at the thermometer to know it was well below zero. A brutal wind was pushing the wind-chill even lower. We trudged up snaking switchbacks for a couple hours, with the inky black night cut only by our headlamps. Our oxygen-starved brain cells mustered just enough consciousness to follow the climbers ahead of us. The higher up your go; the lower your IQ.

When we stopped for a sorely-need breather, one of the doctors confided, "Greg, I think I am third-spacing my water." In mountain parlance, that means that instead of the water being safely in Space #1 (your stomach) or Space #2 (your bladder), it has mischievously found its way into either your lungs or your brain—Space #3.

It was the Mountain Sickness story. The only sure cure would have been to turn around and head back down the mountain. But the trail was dark and steep and dangerous.

"Why do you think you're third-spacing?" I asked, not wanting to turn back.

"Because I haven't had to pee in hours," he replied. Normally, that would be unusual for a couple old guys like us, especially since we had taken care to hydrate well.

"Do you have a headache?" I asked, in my best diagnostician voice.

"No."

"Having trouble breathing?"

"No."

"I think you're OK," I concluded, realizing that I was diagnosing the doctor when such a practice was probably absurd. In *retrospect*, I felt I rested my advice on three facts:

1. If he were really sick, he should have had a headache or breathing problems;

2. High on Kili, like on most major mountains, climbers travel through an arctic desert. It's easy to breathe out a lot of water in the ultra-dry environment. Indeed, we were told to avoid breathing through our mouths in order to conserve water;[1]

3. It would have been very risky to reverse course on the mountain. Any climber will tell you: you're much more likely to die descending than ascending.

The *truth* is that we both wanted to get to the top pretty badly. And, sometimes, if you wait for the perfect story before you move, the perfect story never comes. Only afterwards did it occur to me that perhaps the doctor's own expertise might have been his biggest enemy on the mountain. He wasn't being silly; he was being smart. He knew, far better than I did, the symptoms and the implications; he just needed someone to tell him another story. Thanks in part to the new story, we both felt better—and we both made it safely up and home.

## How Far to Run?

The story that moves you down the road doesn't have to be a long or complicated one. Once, as a young athlete, my daughter Lee asked me "how far should I run?" before she went out for a training run. "Run until you're tired," I replied. "And then run home." More than 15 years later, I noticed that she wore a head band with that simple sentence written on it. "It was great advice," she says.

Turns out, it's a good answer to the question, "When should I stop moving forward?". Many people stop when they're feeling tired. Others will "turn around" in anticipation of being tired later. Whether you're walking across the country, pushing through the jungle or just trying to get a work assignment done, not "turning around" until you're genuinely tired has value. It's not how you know when you're done; it's how you know when you're *half-way* done. Think of the advantages:

> **"Run until you're tired," I replied. "And then run home."**

⚡ *It means that your horizon extends beyond "tired."* Many people want to quit when they're tired, but that's usually way too early. You will often be tired—mentally and physically—well before you've reached your limit.

⚡ If you don't turn around until you're tired, *you'll find that you'll run further each time.* Why? Because you're getting in better shape—mentally and physically—and you'll be able to tolerate more and more before "tired" sets in.

⚡ *You'll often be surprised how far you can really go.* We have a very poor idea of what our real limits are.

⚡ *Half-way is often the point in any exercise where you are most tired.* I often find that knowing that I am heading home can magically re-energize me. Indeed, I am often very strong and fast toward the end of endurance events.

In his business best-seller *Good to Great: Why Some Companies Make the Leap and Others Don't*, Jim Collins tells story after story of how highly-successful companies (some of which no longer exist[2]) became truly great. But the last story of the book isn't about a business; it's about a high school cross-country team.

The team has a very simple story: "We run best at the end." That means at the end of a practice, at the end of a race, or at the end of the season. Their coaches reinforced the story at every practice. They even counted the competitors passed in races *after* the team ran the first two miles. They gave the runners "head bones," little beads in the shape of skulls, based on who they caught at the *end*—when the pain was the greatest and the effort most important. The runners on the team internalized the story completely. The result: championship after championship.[3]

> **Each of us can look back at life and spotlight a story that made or broke us.**

## Change Your Story, Change Your Life

Each of us can look back at life and spotlight a story that made or broke us. These are a few of mine:

⚡ When my guidance counselor told me I had been admitted to Princeton, I suddenly thought, "Well, now I can be anything I want to be."

⚡ When I was at the peak of my journalistic career, covering economics for *The Wall Street Journal* in Washington, I decided to quit without another job but with a vision, "To do what I can to make the world better."

⚡ When my first child was born, I realized, "I am a father. I will give this child every opportunity I can, just like my parents did for me."

⚡ When I turned 50, remembering that my father had died at 58, I declared, "I will be in better shape when I am 60 than I am at 50."

Each story was a hinge in my personal history. It opened certain doors and closed others. Once you tell yourself certain stories you can never be the same again. Change your story; change your life.

## EnergyThink: What Are Your Big Stories?

We are all carrying thousands of stories. Some are high energy, some are low; some generate "good" energy; some "bad." Here are the subjects of The Big Stories:

- ⚡ Work

- ⚡ Family

- ⚡ Health

- ⚡ Happiness

- ⚡ Friends.[4]

For example, if someone asks you, "how are you feeling?", the first answer might be "fine." Does that *really* mean, "I am filled with joy on this beautiful day" or "Well, I'm not dead yet" or "No point in telling you, you can't help me anyway"?

What do you think? Take just a minute or two and write down your "story" for each of the Big Five categories above. You might be shocked by what you discover: it might be why you're feeling unbalanced.

- ⚡ What are your "big" stories that shape your life? Are they realistic? Are they positive?

- ⚡ How accurate are they? Remember: most stories have both a negative and a positive "truth" to them. Which are you selecting?

- ⚡ Which stories do you need to change to live a fuller, higher energy life?

- ⚡ Does "run until you're tired…and then run home" work for you? Recall the last time you felt more energy toward the end of a project, game or exercise.

# 16

## A Little Brain Surgery Might Help Your ANTs

— — — — — — — — — — — — — — — —

**"I once was lost, but now am found,
Was blind but now I see." —The Hymn *Amazing Grace***

— — — — — — — — — — — — — — — —

THE SENSATION OF "KNOWING" SOMETHING THAT IS NOT INTUITIVELY obvious is exactly the mind-bending exercise I'm asking you to bring to our discussion of energy. That's because our traditional concepts of time and energy are deeply ingrained. And it's very hard to change our minds about them.

Surgery might help, though. It helped Diane VanDeren become one of the premier ultra-distance runners in the world. Plagued by epileptic seizures, she underwent an operation that removed a plum-sized portion of her brain. The procedure stopped her seizures, but it also removed her sense of time.

So when she competes in foot races that can last for days and span hundreds of miles, she has very little idea of how long she has been running. As a result, she doesn't "know" that she should feel tired. The farther she runs, the more miles she forgets. Her record is impressive. A few highlights:

⚡ In 2009, she was the first woman finisher in the Yukon Arctic 430 mile race;

⚡ The year before, she was first overall in the 300-mile version of the race;

⚡ In 2006, she finished first overall in two 100-mile races, one in Montana and one in California.

Even though losing track of time makes her everyday life challenging, there are compensations when it comes to using her energy in competition. "The benefit is that you feel freedom," she says in a video I show in my seminars. "You feel light. You feel vibrant. You feel energetic."[1]

It's not "proof" by any means, but her experience suggests that if we're not carrying the "burden" of our perception of time, we can go further, longer, easier. It's seems so simple...and it is.

But it's not easy, mostly because of those ingrained perceptions. For example, from my perspective over the handlebars of a bicycle, my world may look very different from yours. The hill that you easily surmount behind the wheel of a car can be a major challenge for me. Boring back country roads that take you out of your way are my favorite haunts. The bump in the road you barely notice could send me into the ditch.

## ANTs, TST and the Close Pass

"What do you think," people sometimes ask, "when a driver passes you by inches instead of feet?" It's a good question because it happens to me on almost every ride. And it's a huge ANT, an Automatic Negative Thought. Riding across the country, it happened scores of times, often by a big truck on a lonely road with help many miles away. It's like this: imagine you're walking down the street and a shady stranger coming towards you draws a gun and points it at you. As he passes, though, he tucks it back in his holster. Again and again.

> If we're not carrying the "burden" of our perception of time, we can go further, longer, easier.

What do I think? I think of my friend Tom Steinert-Threlkeld. TST was killed on his bicycle by a hit-and-run driver a few miles from home a few years ago. I had ridden with Tom in several states and even Italy. He had a bottomless energy bucket. No matter how tired he was, his mood never flagged. His trademark cackle of a laugh could break glass—and cut through whatever funk his friends happened into.

At his memorial service, we cycling buddies walked his riderless bike at the head of a procession of mourning family and friends. For us, it could have been a reason to stop riding. It was a gigantic ANT. But none of us gave up the bike.

For me, Tom's story is an inspiration to *keep* riding. I will always remember the sheer joy he experienced on his bike—and shared with his friends. Tom never ventured out without a camera. His countless photos document his sense of adventure, humor and whimsy.

Perhaps, if he never rode a bike, Tom would be alive today. When I think of him, though, I remember author John Shedd's famous quotation: "A ship in harbor is safe, but that is not what ships are built for."

## Seeing the Blind Spots

Blind spots can mean life or death. Tom died because a driver didn't see him until it was too late. We miss things hidden in plain sight. We tend not to see our own mistakes. We assume that others see the world as we do. The Talmud, which wasn't written yesterday, observed: "We don't see things as they are. We see them as *we* are."

Great examples of the Talmud's line are everywhere. People still smoke, even though they know it causes cancer and heart attacks. "It won't happen to me!" is the reasoning. And they still buy lottery tickets, a government tax on folks who don't understand math. "It could happen to me!" is what they think. In cycling, it's the age-old debate over whether riders should wear helmets.

> **"Our negative and critical thoughts are like Velcro... whereas our positive and joyful thoughts are like Teflon."**

As someone who's landed on his head more than once, I would never get on a bike without a helmet. In the early days of my biking career, I wore the traditional leather "head net helmet"—and bumped my head with it on. After that, I started wearing a hockey helmet, even though I was the only one in my club to do so. Over the years, I've upgraded—and cracked—a few helmets. There's nothing like going over the handlebars and rolling over on your head to make a helmet believer of you.

And yet there are riders who will argue that helmets are dangerous, for a variety of specious reasons. There's even some shoddy "research" that implies that drivers will pass closer to riders with helmets and that helmeted riders are less cautious.[2] It's a little like arguing that smokers are more healthy because they don't engage in dangerous activities like running marathons.

Franciscan Richard Rohr likes to say, "Our negative and critical thoughts are like Velcro, they stick and hold; whereas our positive and joyful thoughts are like Teflon, they slide away. We have to deliberately choose to hold onto positive thoughts."[3] In other words, our thinking is naturally unbalanced. Here's the unbalanced way I *used to* think before I changed my mind about energy:

⚡ **I can't do this.** This is an ANT, an "Automatic Negative Thought." We all have lots of these crawling around inside our heads. Our mothers, fathers, teachers, coaches, leaders, superiors and peers put them there. In the beginning, it was for our own safety. That's why "NO" is the first word we learn.[4]

⚡ **I don't have enough time.** I like to think of this as both true and false at the same "time." Nobody ever has enough time. Think of Queen Elizabeth I's last words: "All my possessions for a moment of time." Unlike her, however, you are not dead. So you have time.

⚡ **I don't have enough energy.** This one is almost invariably true if you mean "I don't have enough energy... yet." You also probably don't have enough gas in your car to drive 1,000 miles without stopping. You solve that problem by putting more gas in the tank; you just get more energy. That's the wonderful thing about energy. Unlike time, you can almost always get more.

⚡ **I could do this, but I will need chemical help.** For this, you need to recognize the "bull" in Red Bull Energy Drink, Starbucks Coffee, sugary soft drinks, diet pills, amphetamines, fad diets, and all similar "solutions." Yes, they do give you a short-term lift, but then you're worse off because your energy crashes. I confess I have shamelessly resorted to a Coke and a Twinkie to get me through the last 10 miles of a long ride. But these are not the energy boosts we will be recommending in this book.

> **We will draw on the most incredible pharmacopeia known to science.**

Instead, we will draw on the most incredible pharmacopeia known to science: the profound and often mysterious workings of the human brain.

## EnergyThink: What Are Your Automatic Negative Thoughts (ANTs)?

Speaking of ANTs, many years ago when I was in grad school, a professor told the story of a certain species of ant that could find its way through the densest jungle. Because the ant could recognize its own scent and the scent of its fellow ants, it could wander off in search of food and, once the food was found, trace its scent back to its ant mound. Sometimes, however, the ants are trapped on an open space, like a road, in a rainstorm that washes away all the scent. Then, they form a circle and follow each other around and around until they die. Does that remind you of anything?

⚡ What are the patterns that shape your life?

⚡ Do they give you good energy or take it away?

⚡ Where are your "blind spots"?

⚡ What are the ANTs that drive your life?

# 17

# Focus, Form, Flow:
# Disciplines of the Elite Mind

---

"Ready are you? What know you of ready? For eight
hundred years have I trained Jedi.... A Jedi must
have the deepest commitment, the most serious
mind. This one, a long time have I watched. All
his life has he looked away... to the future, to the
horizon. Never his mind on *where* he was.... Hmm?
On *what* he was doing." —Yoda, *Star Wars*

---

TO SOME, WATCHING THE TOUR DE FRANCE IS MUCH THE SAME AS watching golf on TV. Do you know what golfers do? They hit the ball. Over and over. Sometimes, they hit it hard. Sometimes, soft. Sometimes, it goes here. Sometimes, it goes there. Ultimately, it always winds up in the hole. There are no diving catches in the end zone. There are no goalie acrobatics. There are no incredible "swishes" from mid-court. It's why I don't watch golf.

In the Tour de France, a bunch of skinny guys on bikes pedal around France. For days. Sometimes, they go uphill. Sometimes, they go downhill. The scenery is better than golf. But it's pedal, pedal and more pedal.

Yet I find the Tour fascinating. The reason is probably the same reason that golfers watch the U.S. Open. I'm watching the focus, the form and the flow of the athletes. It's all about balance... in so many different ways.

The merging of focus, form and flow—the characteristics of the elite mind—with mental energy is what makes champions champions:

⚡ **Focus.** The best riders have that Samurai air about them. They wield their feather-light machines like warriors with razor-sharp swords. They seem both immune to and energized by the pressure.

⚡ **Form.** The pros have a way of becoming one with their bicycles. It is not only the product of countless hours "busting ass" (to use a Lance term) but also tweaking their form in wind tunnels to achieve near flawless aerodynamics.

⚡ **Flow.** The natural grace of the peloton as the pack winds its way through the mountains is tantamount to the beauty of a river moving smoothly along its banks. It's the sum total of each rider's "flow" on his bike. For the riders, the sport can be both incredibly exhausting and excruciatingly painful. And, clearly, they're having a great time.

## The Fight for Focus in a Noisy World

As I dashed to the airport to catch my flight on my way to the Texas Time Trials a few years ago, I could feel the stress of logistics smother any semblance of focus. A frantic week of out-of-town consulting, late nights and early mornings was not what I needed. Besides, I still had to fly to Texas, rent a car, pick up the bike, drive several hours, check into a hotel, re-assemble the bike, shop for supplies and manage a few hours of sleep before the race start. Not exactly perfect preparation to ride 500 miles in less than 40 hours.

How to muster enough focus to be ready and fresh on a starting line only a few hours away?

As I sat on the plane, catching my breath, I resolved to make the enforced peacefulness of the flight as regenerating as possible. The first step, was to go to "Ashokan Farewell"[1] on my smart phone. It's my "cool down" song of choice. I plugged the earphones into my ears, set the tune on repeat and lost myself in the sweet, mournful sounds of the fiddle and the guitar. Although it was written in 1982, the tune is reminiscent of the Civil War era. It is featured in Ken Burns' *The Civil War* TV series.

> **As the pen scratches softly across the paper, it says to me "slow down and think."**

Once my heart rate had returned to about 50 beats a minute or so, I took out my fountain pen. Such old writing tools are not only obsolete, but they are downright dangerous on planes where a change in cabin pressure can leave you with a lap full of ink. But as the pen scratches softly across the paper, it says to me "slow down and think." It brings back fond memories of my childhood when school desks still had inkwells.

I wrote, slowly...

- ⚡ Relaaaaxxxxx and breathe.
- ⚡ I will do this. I will do this.
- ⚡ Steady. Steady.
- ⚡ Flying. Energy. Energy. Flying. Good energy. Flying above the road.
- ⚡ Control the hills. Up & down. Up & down. Watch the heart rate on the hills.
- ⚡ Momentum. Good momentum.
- ⚡ Drink. Eat. Breathe. Roll.
- ⚡ Easy. Very easy. Nice and easy.
- ⚡ Peaceful, peaceful, peaceful.
- ⚡ The story, deep inside, is strong.
- ⚡ Warm and loose. Warm and loose.
- ⚡ Let's go! *Andiamo!*

By the time, the plane landed, my focus was back. I wasn't ready yet, but I was on my way. I had re-balanced.

How to wrest focus back when everything and everybody is trying to take it from you?

- ⚡ **Develop "peaceful places" where you can go.** Sometimes, these are geographic locations. I wrote a lot of this book at my favorite retreat on the Potomac River. Sometimes, though, you can make a peaceful place anywhere... like on an airplane.
- ⚡ **Meditation works.** Often, the "peaceful place" is inside.
- ⚡ **Music helps.** The image of Olympic athletes wearing headphones before their events is common.
- ⚡ **Training.** If you don't practice focus, it won't happen. Do it enough, and it becomes a habit.

## Form Funnels Your Energy

I remember, as if yesterday, the first time I sat on a real racing bike. One of the guys in my dorm had a white Peugeot 10-speed and offered me the opportunity to ride it around the quad. It was like crack. I was instantly hooked. That was 1969. I've been riding thousands of miles a year since then. Someday, maybe I'll get my form right.

Every sport, including life, has its own form. Sometimes, the form can change radically, like when Olympic Gold Medalist Dick Fosbury invented his famous back-first-over-the-bar "flop" in 1965 and changed high jumping forever.[2]

The purpose of form is to direct your energy—in all its flavors—as efficiently as possible. When you're going to ride a bicycle 500 miles at a stretch, as I did in Texas, even the tiniest changes can have a big impact.

Like when my saddle broke. I was only about 80 miles into the race when my saddle collapsed, tipping me to one side. Talk about loss of balance. It's difficult to describe to a non-rider the disaster a broken saddle implies. On long rides, microscopic differences in position on the bike can make enormous differences in performance and comfort. Some riders go all their lives without finding the *perfect* saddle position. I have paid $300 to a bike fit specialist to adjust my saddle forward less than a centimeter... and it was well worth the price. Also, riders will easily spend that much to get the "perfect" saddle for them. The reason is pretty obvious: ultra-distance riders spend a loooong time on the saddle.

> **Every sport, including life, has its own form.**

So, with a broken saddle, I was looking at a form game-ender. Both my saddle and my form were gone in a single crunch. Even if I could go on, I was sure to suffer extra knee, back, and neck pain. Fortunately, friends scrounged some old saddles, and after a couple changes, I found one that worked fairly well. Thanks to them, I recovered enough form—and balance—to ride 500 miles in just 40 hours.[3]

How do you find "good form"? Obviously, it depends on what the object of the form is, but there some obvious places to look:

⚡ **A coach.** Usually form begins with guidance from an experienced mentor who can look at you dispassionately and give unvarnished advice.

Jim Loehr, who wrote *The Power of Full Engagement*, coaches both athletes and executives.

⚡ **Energy buddies** who care about you and are willing to support your quest for form. They could help you with everything from a better driver swing to a better resume cover letter.

⚡ **Self-help books and videos** can be a good second choice and they are often readily available.

⚡ **Videotaping yourself in action.** Since every smart phone is a video recorder it has never been easier or less expensive to see yourself as others see you. Don't practice your presentation in front of a mirror... practice in front of your phone instead. Practicing in front of a mirror is almost counterproductive. Think about it: the one person you're *not* going to see during your presentation is you!

⚡ **Yoga** and other activities that are heavily form-driven will often yield an "aura" that will spread to other activities.

⚡ **Practice. Practice. Practice.** To quote the great Eddy Merckx: "Ride as much or as little, or as long or as short as you feel. But ride."

Notice that, in our modern world, we work hard to *get around* form, since it takes time, energy and practice to acquire, polish and keep it. There is a never-ending hunt for a short-cut, for "cheap grace." Usually, technology is ready with an answer. Red Bull is a short-cut for "real" energy. Texting "TU" is a short-cut for a thank-you note. Missing your daughter's first school play but wiring her roses instead is a short-cut for being a parent.

As an archer, I began my hobby with modern technology: a compound bow. It's a complicated, heavy device of pulleys and cables, made heavier with a stabilizing weight and sights, like those on a gun. With very little practice, I could shoot it fairly well. I would aim, aim, aim...hold my breath...release the string. The bow would go "thunk" and the arrow would hit the target.

Then a friend suggested I try a traditional bow. It's a spectacularly simple device: a stick and a string. It shoots another stick, like archers have done for thousands of years. You really don't aim... there are no sights...you look at the target. You draw and shoot and your brain automatically calculates the distance and the trajectory. It's like a quarterback passing to a receiver or a pitcher finding the strike zone. Shooting a traditional bow demands good form. It only works if you do it over and over and over again, thousands of times. And then, it only works if you are concentrating.

The release of a traditional bow, however, is a silent, Zen-like whisper that speaks to a special part of your brain. It is the same sensation that our ancestors' ancestors felt. It has a mystical, form-based feeling that is like no other. Shooting a bow may actually be in our DNA, like a sense of direction.

> **Every piece of technology gives us a choice.**

Every piece of technology gives us a choice. Socrates bemoaned how writing reduced the power of memory...because people didn't have to remember as much if they wrote down information. Replace your sense of direction with a GPS and your sense of direction goes away. Take the elevator instead of the stairs and your legs become weaker. Replace form with a short-cut; form goes away.

## When You're In Flow, Anything Goes

The great psychologist Mihaly Csikszntmihalyi fathered the concept of flow—of being so immersed in an activity that you are completely absorbed by it. In flow, there is a rush of joyful energy in the task and the effort seems minimal. In his book with Susan Jackson, *Flow in Sports: The Keys to Optimal Experiences and Performances,* they use the words of a world-class cyclist, "Simon," to describe the "Nine Fundamental Dimensions of Flow." It's much cooler to see how the biker describes flow than to give you another list. In the outline below, the cyclist describes how he experienced each of the dimensions—and especially balance—on the bike:

1. **The Challenge-Skills Balance.** "There's a certain point at which you can convert stressful situations to challenges...which is where the flow sort of triggers off and you go, and it is like nothing is going to get in the way."

2. **Action-Awareness Merging.** "It doesn't seem like you're sitting on a bike.... It's like you're part of this machine that you were born with, and it's how you move."

3. **Clear Goals.** "You can almost touch or know that you can predict the outcome of the event before it actually happens."

4. **Unambiguous Feedback.** "What gear you're riding; what position you're sitting in; where the second, third, fourth, and fifth riders are sitting in the bunch; what numbers are in the breakaway; how many riders there are in front of you—all these things take your attention."

5. **Concentration on the Task at Hand.** "I rode four hours one day in the rain and sleet, and I don't think I remember anything other than the white line on the road, going underneath for four hours. And the guy's wheel in front of me. For four hours, that's all I remember."

6. **Sense of Control.** A feeling of "unshatterable self-esteem"—that he could take on anything and be able to get through it.

7. **Loss of Self-consciousness.** "You can let go of worrying about how others see you and whether you have what it takes to be successful."

8. **Transformation of Time.** In describing an event that took 11 seconds, "It felt like you'd slowed everything down and made sure everything was right...it felt real quick, but everything felt slow at the same time." Sometimes, hours pass like minutes; minutes like seconds—and the other way around.

9. **Autotelic Experience.** The experience is so rewarding, people do it for its own sake. "There's no experience in sport that is as exhilarating or rewarding as being in flow. That's what makes me keep riding, knowing that I might get it again."

"Flow provides a glimpse of perfection," the authors say, "which is why we seek it again and again once we attain it."

For me, I most commonly feel flow on my bike, but I've experienced it in front of a class, in intense conversations, on the archery range with my bow, and even doing very routine tasks like cleaning my house.

If you want to see what truly intense flow looks like, check out a teenager playing video games.

## Don't Fight the Flow

Arthur Conan Doyle, creator of Sherlock Holmes, described the feeling of "flow" when he said, "When the spirits are low, when the day appears dark, when work becomes monotonous, when hope hardly seems worth having, just mount a bicycle and go out for a spin down the road, without thought on anything but the ride you are taking."

Ultra distance cycling relies heavily on flow. What does *not* work is thinking about every mile, every hill, every pedal turn and, especially, how far you have to go. When the brain turns toward the immediate discomfort and away from the joy of the overall experience, flow vanishes.

In my energy seminars, people will often ask me how I can spend 24 or more hours on a bicycle when they couldn't even imagine doing that in a car, much less at their jobs. My response to that is simply "flow." I like it.[4]

Watching great athletes do their thing can be flow-inspiring. The player or team that suddenly catches fire during a game and scores repeatedly and (apparently) easily is often harnessing flow. Think of ballerinas, figure skaters, Julius Irving in basketball, Michael Phelps in swimming, Yo-Yo Ma on the cello, John Belushi on *Saturday Night Live*.

The most common place to find flow is in doing something you *love* to do. Flow is often a consequence of living your mission, which we will address in detail later in this book.

## EnergyThink: Finding Focus, Form and Flow in Your Life

Where are focus, form and flow in your life? Think about activities that require all your attention (focus), those that require you to keep your balance in special ways (form), and those that can make you lose track of time (flow).

⚡ Identify your *focus* activities. Would sharpening your focus help you do them better? How would you do that? Are they even the right activities on which to focus?

⚡ Identify your activities that demand good *form*. How would you evaluate your form? Do you want to improve it? How?

⚡ *Flow* is believed by some to be one of the key elements of happiness. We'll explore that more later, but, for now, think about how you feel when you're in flow. Would you like more of it?

# 18

## MacGvyering a More Resourceful *UP*

------------------------------------------------

**"The bag's not for what I take, Colson. It's for what I find along the way." —TV Hero Angus MacGyver**

------------------------------------------------

RESOURCEFULNESS, OFTEN MISLABELED "CREATIVITY," IS A HALLMARK of great intellectual energy.

Although it has been decades since secret agent Angus MacGyver did his thing across the TV screens of America, he left an indelible stamp as the Patron Saint of Extricating Oneself from a Certain Death and Succeeding in the Impossible Mission by Using Only Duck Tape, a Paper Clip and a Swiss Army Knife.

Although MacGyver is often invoked when somebody says "We need to think outside the box," that is improper usage, in my humble opinion. MacGyver's genius was *not* in thinking *outside* the box, but rather in recognizing that there was more *inside* the box than anybody thought. His ability to see potential where others only saw obstacles is one of the most valuable intellectual energy skills. He's not as creative as he is *resourceful*.

The MacGyver approach that delighted TV audiences is simple:

**1.** Believe no problem is unsolvable, no matter how dire it seems;

**2.** Keep a cool head—and use it to understand clearly what is happening;

**3.** Boost energy;

**4.** Connect the dots... differently;

**5.** Adapt!

## Believe It: You Have Everything You Need

When my bike breaks on races in remote locations, I have my own MacGyver mantra: "Everything you need to fix this is right there on the road." Surprisingly, it often is. The idea not only restores confidence and fights panic, it opens my eyes to discovering solutions I would never have dreamed.

The most dramatic example of this occurred when I broke a crank at the pedal 50 miles into a 250 mile race in a desolate corner of West Virginia. A broken crank is pretty serious when the nearest bike shop is 50 miles away and there are mountains in every direction.

My competitors rolled by, making jokes about a one-legged man in a butt kicking contest. I assumed I was finished. I was wrong.

With no cell service, I was reduced to knocking on doors in the thriving metropolis of Parker Hollow. I didn't have many doors to choose from. Still, I picked the right one: Dorman Parker answered my knock. A big guy in a cutoff sweatshirt, when he appeared I thought I heard banjo music, a la the movie *Deliverance*. He asked the sweaty stranger in Lycra what the problem was. I pointed to the broken bike. He announced, "We can fix that."

I was about to tell him that there was no way he could repair my sophisticated, expensive, hi-tech bike. But I bit my tongue. Good thing I did. Dorman was no backwoods bumpkin. He was a talented mechanic (and a very nice guy) with a MacGyver mind. And he just happened to have a machine shop next to his house. In a jiffy, he MacGyvered a solution I would have never imagined, drilling and tapping a hole in my broken crank and screwing in a pedal from his kid's old mountain bike. It wasn't pretty, but it worked. In no time, I was back on the road, with both my bike and my energy restored.

> I assumed I was finished. I was wrong.

## Is Your Focus Too Narrow?

The MacGyver approach illustrates an important concept about the discipline of focus in a crisis. *Your focus doesn't have to be as narrow as you think.* For some, focus means looking at life through a soda straw. They just see one little piece of the world. This tunnel vision is little more than situational blindness. A good quarterback demonstrates the exact opposite of this condition. Immediately after the snap, he looks for the open receiver—and that often is *not* the receiver he envisioned after leaving the huddle seconds earlier.

One of the best examples of the *right* kind of focus is improv comedy. My daughter, Annie, spent a lot of time studying improv at the Ground Zero of this form of comedy—Second City in Chicago. At the same time, she was working on her MBA down the street at the Kellogg School at Northwestern University.

"You know, Dad," she remarked, "they go together really well." The dual disciplines of business skills and improv vision surely do marry well. If you go to Second City, the alma mater of comedy icons like John Belushi and Gilda Radner (just to name two of many), you can buy a "Yes, And…" T-shirt. "Yes, and" is one of the commandments of improv. It forces you to focus on what your partner on the stage is saying…and build on it. It's way ahead of the "yes…but" that usually finds its way into business (and life) conversations.

In fact, Annie is on the board of Room2Improv, a non-profit that uses improv skills to help returning vets, students and seniors change their stories and re-imagine better lives.

## Adopting the Rules of Improv

These are my favorite rules of improv comedy…almost all of which are about a broader focus that can bring energy to the stage…and your life:

- ⚡ You are all supporting actors. Your prime responsibility is to support.

- ⚡ Save your fellow actor, don't worry about the piece. Try to make your scene partners appear brilliant. Treat everything they say as a gift, even—especially—if it's not what you would have said.

- ⚡ Never underestimate or condescend to your audience.

- ⚡ Trust. Trust your fellow actors to support you; trust them to come through if you lay something heavy on them; trust yourself.

- ⚡ Listen. Pay hyper-close attention to everything that happens on stage.

- ⚡ Remember "chivalry"—not clinging to your own idea, your own status, or even your own life as a character. Give up your own ideas when the scene doesn't progress as you had hoped. Chivalry is daring to give up control. Allow yourself to be changed. Be happy to be forced to change.

⚡ "Yes and." Take whatever has been given in the scene so far and build on it. Just build the reality. Don't consciously try to be funny. Cooperate with your scene partners, don't fight them.

⚡ Your mind is your personal Google, your personal search engine. Your brain always gives you something back if you put something in. But don't put in "funny," "clever," "good," "original," etc.

⚡ Commit. Sell it. Put your line out there. Make your choice and let whatever happens happen. Never say a line tentatively, like you need audience approval.

⚡ Come at the highest level you can, as relaxed as you can. Have fun.

> **Take risks. Dare to fail big. Experiment.**

⚡ Take risks. Dare to fail big. Experiment. Do things on stage that you've never done before.

⚡ If you get stuck, put your attention on your scene partners, listen to what they're saying, notice what they're doing, visualize where they are, guess what their character is feeling or needing.[1]

## EnergyThink: How Can You Set Free the MacGyver In You?

It would be a mistake to assume that MacGyvering just happens naturally, without training, practice and experience. Although some people might come by improv juice via their DNA, most of us common folk have to work at it.

For example, on January 15, 2009, US Airways Flight 1549 left LaGuardia Airport in New York City and promptly struck a flock of birds that shut down its engines. Fifty-seven-year-old Captain Chesley B. "Sully" Sullenberger was at the controls. He managed to land the plane safely in the Hudson River, saving the lives of all 155 on board.

Essentially, he "MacGyvered" a safe river landing, something nobody had ever done before, including him. But that doesn't mean he hadn't worked at it. A former fighter pilot, he had been in tight jams before. He had almost 20,000 hours of flying time in passenger jets. He was an airline safety expert and had undoubtedly practiced similar maneuvers during long hours in flight simulators. And he was a glider pilot, so he knew something about flying without an engine.

Go online and listen to him talk with the airport tower before the crash landing. There are several simulations on YouTube. There is not a trace of anxiety in his voice. If you'd like to be that cool in a crisis, there are four key ways to do the "mental pushups" to make you a better MacGyver: prepare, be more creative, visualize success and positive self-talk.

1. **Preparation.** It's impossible to be prepared for everything; but could you be ready for *anything*? "Open" minds and systems can accommodate the unexpected better than hardened, closed systems.

2. **Creativity.** Perhaps the biggest challenge to creativity is allowing for it. How can you give yourself and others permission to be creative?

3. **Visualization.** Jack Nicklaus once said, "I never missed a putt in my mind."[2] You're more likely to get the success that you foresee. Can you foresee more success in the future?

4. **Self-talk.** Like the stories that change your life, you have to *believe* your self-talk. What should you be saying to yourself?

# 19

# Humility: The Intellectual Bridge to Emotional *UP*

---

**"Humility is not thinking less of yourself. It's thinking of yourself less." —C.S. Lewis**

---

WANT TO FEEL VULNERABLE? RIDE THROUGH SOUTHERN TIMBER country on a bicycle.

I'm sure loggers are sensible, courteous, intelligent drivers—when they are *not* behind the wheel of a semi, hauling a truckload of freshly felled trees. When they are, they are so dangerous that some states actually post temporary signs warning "trucks on the road." The loggers drive hell-bent-for-leather on rolling, two-lane, shoulderless country roads, cranking their big rigs hard on the downhills to gather momentum for the ups.

"This, foolish rider, is *their* road," said the voice in my head (and the angry roar of the diesel behind me) as I made my way across the country in 2015. Just to underline their point, the truckers often passed close, sometimes close enough to reach out and touch, spewing bark chips in their wakes.

Loggers are an Official Threat, along with lightning, sunstroke, ice, steep mountain roads, potholes, deer, rain-slick steel bridges, storm grates, and other assorted fauna and flora, flotsam and jetsam, that just plain don't care whether you live or die. I try to watch for, but not worry too much about, those things. That's mostly because:

⚡ I can't do anything about them;

⚡ If I did worry, it would cost intellectual and emotional energy;

⚡ Then I might not ride.

## What *Is* Worth Thinking About:
## Greg's Four Rules of the Long Road

Every cyclist hoping to ride across America needs a healthy ego. One has to believe one can do this monumental feat...or one will surely fail. One also has to come to grips with the indisputable fact that one is much more likely to fail because of one's own vulnerabilities than all of the Official Threats put together.

In other words, you're more likely to screw yourself than be screwed by somebody or something else. In other words, *humility is power.* It's the best protection you can get...against yourself. In a few words, value your vulnerabilities and honor *Greg's Four Rules of the Long Road*:

1. You *will* do something really, really stupid;

2. Testosterone *kills;*

3. Sweat the *small stuff;*

4. It's all about your "*knees.*"[1]

> **Humility is power.**

## Something Stupid: It's Inevitable

A long-time riding buddy, Phil Feldman, has a name for it: "The Century Stupids." It refers to the mistakes that are common after a "century" or 100-mile ride. The brain runs on sugar and, frequently, riders' blood sugar is pretty low after a long effort.

Once, toward the end of a 24-hour, 270-mile ride enhanced by pouring rain and hypothermic temperatures, a riding buddy punctured. We were all cold, wet, tired and miserable and we fumbled through the repair. The finish was a long, steep hill and we eagerly speed down it. At the finish, we discovered that his tire was, once again, flat. We hadn't thought to check for glass stuck in the tire. If the hill had come just a few hundred yards later in the ride, we might have ended in a crash.

Sometimes, the consequences are downright comical. On a racing bike, the pedals are a little like ski bindings. The rider's shoes "clip" into them so they don't accidentally slide off. To release the shoe from the pedal, the rider merely twists his heel away from the bike. Racing Paris-Brest-Paris in 2007, I reached my hotel at the end of a long and difficult day of more than 200 soggy miles. I had picked up my overnight bag at a checkpoint and it was slung over my shoulder.

At the door of the hotel, I stopped my bicycle, but forgot to unclip the pedals. I fell over, pinned to the gutter by the bike and the bag. I couldn't move. Eventually, somebody from the hotel bar appeared and unraveled me, red-faced, from the tangle.

The moral of the story: *Be extra careful when you're extra tired.*

## Testosterone Kills Its Victims: That Would Be *You*

If you ever watch a serious bike race, you might notice a faint cloud that hangs over the pack like a gray halo. That's not dust. It's testosterone, the hormone of dominance. There is a good reason that they called the great champion Eddy Merckx "The Cannibal." Most riders just plain want to demonstrate they can eat other riders for lunch.

This condition often worms its way down to even "friendly" club rides, as infected cyclists strive to drop each other on steep hills or shred the pack's legs with sustained bursts of speed. I confess that, locked deep within my Italian genes, their *might* be a *slight* tendency for me to do this, but I am fighting it in my old age.

As you might suspect, the testosterone tendency is accelerated if there are women in the group, especially if they are competitive (and they frequently are in serious cycling circles). On my trip across the country, there were 16 riders: 15 men and one woman. She was exceptionally strong, 20 years younger than me, and 40 pounds lighter.

> **Don't let your hormones write checks your body can't cash.**

It didn't take me long to figure out I wouldn't be riding with her much. Some of the guys who tried to keep up with her learned a painful lesson in humility!

The moral of the story: *Don't let your hormones write checks your body can't cash.*

## Sweat the Small Stuff: It Will Save You

A powerful intellectual energy tool is list-making. No good pilot would fly without the pre-flight checklist. Countless lives have been saved by hospital checklists. I never travel to an important cycling event without my list. There is nothing worse than discovering you left your shoes, your helmet, your sunglasses or some other vital item home.

Compared to cars and computers, a bicycle is a pretty simple machine. But like any precision tool, it rewards careful maintenance. And, of course, it will break from time to time. I carry with me all the tools and parts needed for most common on-the-road mishaps.

Speaking of sweat, water is an often-overlooked detail. I mentioned its powers earlier in the book, but on the long road it can mean much more than just energy—it can mean life itself. Some riders will not bring enough water. Some will bring it but forget to drink it. I've ridden through the deserts of the West. I've ridden rides of hundreds of miles where temperatures oozed over 100 degrees day after day. I've seen many riders taken to emergency rooms for dehydration because they neglected the smallest detail: a few simple sips.

The moral of the story: Remember Ben Franklin's saying:

For the want of a nail the shoe was lost,
For the want of a shoe the horse was lost,
For the want of a horse the rider was lost,
For the want of a rider the battle was lost,
For the want of a battle the kingdom was lost,
And all for the want of a horseshoe-nail.

## It's All About Your "Knees"

The most vulnerable parts of my body (that I care to mention) are my knees. When I rode across the country in 2004 my knees were killing me. That's not a big surprise, since riding coast to coast involves about a million pedal turns, more or less. Some riders had to abandon because of knee pain. Others, like me, suffered through unhappily.

For many months after that ride, knee pain continued to plague me.

Once burned, twice shy. For my 2015 trip, a lot of my preparation concentrated on knees. I installed lower gears on the bike, shortened my cranks, lost 20 pounds, got a professional bike fit, wrapped the knees with KT tape, did hours of yoga to strengthen them, and took it easy on the climbs.

It paid off: very little knee pain, despite long, long days in the saddle.

We all have "knees"—literally and metaphorically. These are the weak spots that will derail our best efforts. We're tempted to ignore them and hope they go away. But they can be just like Ben Franklin's nail. Identifying these "spoilers" in advance and doing something about them can make all the difference.

The moral of the story: *Please your knees.*[2]

## EnergyThink: What Are Your "Rules of the Road"?

Humility is the bridge between intellectual energy and emotional energy because it helps us think about how we would feel and respond if the unthinkable happened. The famous last words, "That would never happen to me," represent the hubris that goes before the fall.

⚡ What are your "Rules of the Road" that will protect you from yourself?

⚡ What might you do that is stupid?

⚡ Where might your ego get the best of you?

⚡ Which details will derail your trip? What goes on your checklist?

⚡ Which are your most valuable vulnerabilities?

# PART FIVE

# Harnessing Emotional Energy

## 20

# Energy Vampires: They Suck *UP*

--- --- --- --- --- --- --- --- --- --- --- --- --- --- ---

**"Nobody cares how much you know until they
know how much you care." —Teddy Roosevelt**

--- --- --- --- --- --- --- --- --- --- --- --- --- --- ---

EMOTIONAL ENERGY IS MOOD-DRIVEN; IT'S ABOUT YOUR FEELINGS, especially fear or lack of it.

My friend Carol Bell is one of the best Randonneurs I know. In fact, her smiling face graces the cover of the official handbook published by Randonneurs USA, the American[1] governing body for Randonneuring, a version of ultra-distance cycling. A "Kiwi," she has raced in her native New Zealand as well as in North America and Europe. As good as she is, she is a time manager. So, in 2007, when we packed off to race Paris-Brest-Paris, she chose the 90-hour, leave-in-the-evening start while I chose the 84-hour, leave-the-next-morning-after-a-good-night's-sleep option.

Around 2:30 on the afternoon of our first day of racing, I caught up with her. She was *not* happy.

"Carol, how are you doing?" I asked in my annoyingly cheerful way.

"I'm knackered," she replied glumly. After a long night of riding in the rain with no sleep, she was exhausted. "I'm 300 kilometers into a 1200 kilometer event and don't know if I'm going to make it."

"Carol, there's a nice little patisserie right up ahead," I said. "How about we stop and have a little coffee and cake?"

"Oh, no, Greg," she countered. "Don't waste your time on me. You're going to have a really good time."

As soon as she mentioned the "T" word, I knew we needed to stop. It took a little convincing, but we pulled over and had a little party, right on the side of the road, right in the middle of the race. When I left her, she was smiling and we both rode faster.

## "Do Not Be Afraid"

"Fear is the path to the dark side...fear leads to anger...anger leads to hate...hate leads to suffering." Yoda declares in *Star Wars: The Phantom Menace*. The three-fingered green sage is describing the downward spiral of the biggest emotional drain of them all: FEAR.

There is a reason that the most common phrase in the Bible is "Do not be afraid." Usually, the phrase signals something like "Sit tight. A miracle is about to happen." The warning is necessary because it's human nature to cut and run just when the party is getting good. "Scared money doesn't win" is a poker saying almost old enough to be biblical.

Yet the System One Wookie in our heads is fear-driven and strong and very difficult to overcome. Often, this is for our own good; fear is a good survival mechanism. But its energy is often negative. Therefore, it's no surprise that the biggest emotional "sinks," in the end, are all about fear:

⚡ Negative management or communication styles;

⚡ Negative thinking;

⚡ Negative personal matters;

⚡ Negative people.

The antidote to fear is courage. Courage is the ability to do what needs to be done even though you are afraid. Courage is a spiritual *UP* that we'll investigate more thoroughly later. We need fear to survive, but we also need courage to thrive.

> **Energy—both negative and positive—feeds on itself.**

Energy—both negative and positive—feeds on itself. In politics, in battle, in your office, in your home... you can see and feel it everywhere.

## Vampires: "The We're Not Happy Until You're Not Happy" Folks

Speaking of feeding negative energy, let's begin with negative persons, since many of the other sinks originate with them anyway. And let's pick on the most important one first: me (or, in your case, you). Before you protest, please understand that I am not accusing either of us of being all that negative. It's just that we have to live with ourselves all the time. So even little tiny bits of negativity gather compound interest. Now that we've settled that, let's pick on other folks, which is *way* more fun.

Like Lucifer in the Book of Job, negative folks are "going to and fro on the earth, and walking up and down in it." In other words, they're everywhere, tempting you to be afraid of just about anything you dream of doing. They are your Energy Vampires. In my energy seminars, most people want to know what to do about the vampires in their lives.

Because vampires can be so deadly, it's important to be able to spot them—fast! In fact, FAST is a great way to identify them. They...

⚡ **Fear:** and are both scary and afraid. Often, to cover that fear, they do things to make you fear them, too. They will hunt for any point of leverage over you and others that they can find. Sometimes, they are bullies; sometimes, seducers; sometimes, they play victim. They are not always "bad" people from a moral standpoint, but they are always bad for energy—yours, your team's, and your organization's.

> **Because vampires can be so deadly, it's important to be able to spot them—fast!**

⚡ **Avoid:** risk, blame, change, sunlight. Because they are afraid, they will work hard to shift the blame for anything bad to someone else. It's a misguided survival mechanism, right out of their System One Wookie mindset. (See our discussion of System One in Chapter 12.) Because they are System One driven, they abhor change, especially if there is any potential risk to them. Most of all, they fear exposure for what they truly are. They will universally deny being vampires; first, to themselves and, then, to anyone who will listen.

⚡ **Say:** no, negative, nothing, never, not me. These are the "N-words" of energy management. (Consider them the slurs that they are.) "When people become fearful, they recognize and communicate the dangers," says Robert Quinn in *Change the World*. "They do not recognize and communicate the opportunities."[2]

⚡ **Think:** it can't be done. Can you guess why they think that whatever is on the table can't be done? Of course: THERE'S NOT ENOUGH TIME! *Which is why vampires have to live forever!*

On the bike, vampires are easy to spot. Even racing in the dark in foreign countries, where the other riders in the pack speak no known language and you can only see their headlights and tail lights, you can tell a vampire. They can be strong, but they refuse to go to the front to take on the wind and to offer shelter, even briefly, to the other riders. They exude a negative, "elbows out" competitiveness. Sometimes, they'll disrupt the flow, dashing ahead of the pack for no apparent reason. The group often will sprint to catch them, squandering energy. Caught, the vampires will slide back into the peloton, but they will coast and weave, making it difficult for the other riders to draft them. Riding with vampires is much harder than riding with buddies.

## You, the Vampire Slayer

Everybody knows how to dispose of vampires: a stake right through their black little hearts, preferably in broad daylight when they can't do anything about it. While you're fantasizing about that bright prospect, understand that you're probably not going to get away with a clean kill. Still, STAKE might prove a good strategy:

⚡ **Speak "energy" to them.** Since nobody wants to be seen as a vampire, especially vampires, using energy language might be effective. Something like, "Did you realize, Joe, that when you showed up a half hour late for the meeting, you drained energy from the whole group?" Or, perhaps, "Mary, by trashing Phil's idea before he could fully explain it, did you know you sapped all the positive momentum in the room?" Or, even, "Denny, because you didn't do the report you promised, we lost the sale and wasted all the energy everybody put into the case."

⚡ **Take away perverse incentives.** Compensation systems are frequently full of perverse incentives. These are the unintended consequences that work against the very goals the incentives are trying to support. For example, any system that punishes people for making well-intentioned mistakes or taking calculated risks that ultimately fail will quickly extinguish energy. Policies that encourage emotionally draining competition among teams are usually counterproductive. Friendly sales contests

> A couple of buddies can be more positive than one vampire.

and good-natured competition can juice teams. But anything that discourages cooperation or creates win-lose scenarios should immediately be suspect. Business history is full of stories about higher pay leading to worse performance.[3]

⚡ **Acquire "buddies."** If you must work in a space occupied by vampires, having buddies can counteract some of the negative impact. A couple of buddies can be more positive than one vampire. It's usually easier to do a distasteful task (filing would be my best example) if you have friendly company.

⚡ **Kill 'em with kindness.** Because vampirism is fear based, sometimes just being nice to vampires does the trick. Unless they are hardened cases, usually people will respond to good behavior with good behavior. You can certainly out-smile them (it's hard to smile with fangs). But don't waste your energy arguing with them. If you say "Yes...but," they'll suck you right into their trap.

⚡ **Eliminate them.** In the end, if all else fails, they have to go. "But what if the vampire is your boss?" some folks ask. Well, perhaps you have to fire your boss. It's called quitting. (We'll get to that later.)

## Don't Be "4F"

"4F" is a "U.S. Selective Service classification designating a person considered physically, psychologically, or morally unfit for military duty."[4] In energy parlance, "4F" means the weapons that vampires use on us: frustrate, fluster, fatigue and fear.

> **The Vampire Vicious Cycle only breeds more vampires.**

I confess to using them as tactics on cycling competitors. Once, on a 200 kilometer race, my riding partner and I stopped to make a minor repair. The typical, courteous practice in Randonneuring would be for a rider passing us to slow and inquire whether we needed help. But one young stud saw this as an opportunity to beat us more soundly and accelerated by without so much as a word.

My partner wanted to chase him down, which we could have done. But that would have cost extra effort and energy. Instead, we followed him a few hundred yards back. I knew his inability to drop us would be *frustrating* as we tagged along at the edge of his rear view vision.

Then as the course grew more hilly, we slowly closed the gap. We could see him, *flustered*, struggling to hold us off. His form deteriorated steadily as he gritted his teeth to attack every hill.

Eventually, we picked a nice steep hill, when his stressed quads would be in flames and his *fatigue* at the max...and passed him decisively. We knew that, if we crested the hill sufficiently ahead of him we could fly downhill and be well out of sight by the time he reached the top.

Then, not really knowing how far ahead we were, the *fear* that he could not catch us would slow him down. The ploy worked. Although he was probably half my age, he gave up and finished far behind us.

## EnergyThink: Stop the VVC

The Vampire Vicious Cycle (You do it to me; I do it back to you) only breeds more vampires. In *Shakelton's Way: Leadership Lessons from the Great Antarctic Explorer,* Margot Morrell and Stephanie Capparell describe Ernest Shakelton's approach to handling vampires. When his crew was marooned on the ice in Antarctica, there was no easy way to deal with the vampires, but the survival of the whole crew depended on solid morale.

The ship's first officer, Lionel Greenstreet, described Shakelton's tactic of holding his friends close—and his potential enemies even closer. He invited them into his tent: "He collected with him the ones he thought wouldn't mix with the others," Greenstreet said. "They were not so easy to get on with, the ones he had in his tent with him—they were quite a mixed bag."[5]

President Abraham Lincoln adopted the same strategy in creating his cabinet, as described in Doris Kearns Goodwin's classic *Team of Rivals: The Political Genius of Abraham Lincoln.* As President Lyndon Johnson said, "I'd rather have the guy inside my tent pissing out, rather than outside my tent, pissing in."

## EnergyThink: You and Shakelton, Lincoln and Johnson

⚡ Can you adopt the Shakelton-Lincoln-Johnson approach to the vampires you have around you?

⚡ What weapons do the vampires use on you?

⚡ How do they manipulate you?

⚡ How do they prey upon your fears? Which fears?

⚡ What can you do to keep them from doing that to you?

⚡ Vampirism doesn't have to be a two-way street. Just because they do it to you, you don't have to do it to them or others. How can you stop the VVC ?

Paris-Brest-Paris, the world's oldest bicycle race, is the like Olympics of ultra-distance riding. In 2007, Greg finished the 750-mile event in slightly more than 72 hours, despite some of the most miserable weather in the race's history.

Energy buddies John Fuoco and Andrea Matney share a lighter moment. John's unflagging spiritual energy and inspiring character have kept him alive, strong and on the bike despite a long battle with cancer.
*Photo by Greg Conderacci*

Racing a bicycle around Alaska can be challenging mentally and physically, but it's hard to beat the views. The 2013 Big Wild Ride took competitors from Valdez to Fairbanks to Anchorage—more than 750 miles—in less than four days. *Photo by Greg Conderacci*

The desert can be a formidable obstacle on a cross-country ride. Here riders roll through the sand dunes on The PAC Tour Elite Transcontinental in 2015. Long stretches in the desert and mountains are the hallmarks of this 18-day dash from coast to coast that averages 150 miles a day. *Photo by Greg Conderacci*

Even though it's at the Equator, at more than 19,000 feet the summit of Kilimanjaro is a cold and desolate place. In 2006, Greg (far left) stood on the Roof of Africa with this hardy band of climbers and guides.

Greg (pointing) surrounded by "energy buddies." Riding with friends can make even the longest and most difficult challenges far easier. *Photo by Mike Wali*

Tom Steinert-Threlkeld shows off his irrepressible style. Better than most of us, Tom embodied all four kinds of energy—physical, intellectual, emotional and spiritual. Tragically, he was killed on his bicycle by a hit-and-run driver in 2013. *Photo by Greg Conderacci*

Frank Ryan, the CPA and former Marine colonel who walked from coast to coast in 2014, was *Semper Fi* all the way across America. His spiritual energy powered him past many geographic and physical obstacles over his journey of more than 150 days. *Photo by Greg Conderacci*

# 21

# Energy Buddies to the Rescue

— — — — — — — — — — — — — —

**"We few, we happy few. We band of brothers."**
**—William Shakespeare, *Henry V***

— — — — — — — — — — — — — —

EVERYBODY IN MY BIKE CLUB WANTS TO RIDE WITH ANDREA MATNEY. At 2 am, in a driving rain storm, when you're as miserable as a Navy SEAL in Hell Week, Andrea is all smiles and good energy. On a bike, she is the ultimate Energy Buddy.

More than once, she has literally saved my life. The most notable occasion was in 2011, when we were both racing Paris-Brest-Paris for the second time. The first time out, four years earlier, she had contracted pneumonia on the ride and had to retire early. Both her husband Steve and I grew tired of hearing her PBP ("Paris-Brest-Pneumonia") story, so we promised to support her second attempt.

Since I had done well in my first PBP in 2007, I planned on playing the Wise Older Brother who would escort her through the ordeal. Little did I know...

Like 2007, the 2011 version of PBP was wet. We raced through the first day, dodging thunderstorms. At dusk, The Cloud From Hell appeared on the horizon. Black at the top, the cloud was blood red at the bottom from the setting sun. Jagged bolts of lightning etched patterns across it.

We thought we might be able to outrun it. Even though we had ridden hard all day, we added a burst of speed. It wasn't enough. Amid a barrage of lightning, the rain came down in sheets. We rode from doorway to doorway, sheltering from the onslaught as best we could, two bedraggled riders in the storm.

As night came on, the rain intensified, flooding the roads and blinding me. In the dark and wet, my glasses fogged. I groped along the unlit country road more by feel than by sight. Suddenly, with the temperature dropping, my rear tire flatted. Repairing a flat is no fun, even in the sunshine; in the pelting rain it was downright agony.

The worse part was that we could not find what had caused the flat. As any rider knows, putting a new tube in a tire with a hidden piece of glass is inviting another flat. By the light of our head lamps, we searched the inside of the tire: nothing. Shivering in the cold, I persisted in my hunt, knowing we could not afford another flat in this weather. Finally, with my core temperature plummeting, I gave up and mounted the tire.

## Surviving Hypothermia—Thanks to My Energy Buddy

On the road, I was a new man. But not in a good way. The tired but steady rider who stopped to fix the flat was replaced by a hypothermic rider who could barely turn the pedals. Climbing even a modest hill took forever. I weaved back and forth across the road, fighting sleep.

Fortunately, Andrea was fine. Every time I drifted towards the edge of the road she shouted at me, both to keep me on the road and to keep me awake. In the gloom, I focused on her bike's back light and pressed on. When we reached the checkpoint with our rooms for the night, I was stunned by the time. It was much later than I had thought. Somewhere in the night, I had lost three hours.

> **Somewhere in the night, I had lost three hours.**

As we checked in to the overnight, we heard rumors of a cyclist who had been struck and killed by a truck that evening. Later, we learned it was a member of our club. I could only think that, without Andrea helping me through the hypothermia, it could have been me.

## Who's Your Buddy?

Energy buddies come in all varieties. Some will get you through difficult times; some are there to add zest to the good times; some will help you navigate complex tasks; some will help you endure unpleasant ones. They are assistants, coaches, leaders, guides, lovers, planners, organizers, partners, advisers, cheerleaders, jokers, spouses, and, almost always, friends. I hope that this book can be your buddy, too.

Usually, spotting a buddy can be even easier than spotting a vampire. There is a resonance between the two of you, a natural friendliness that says, "we can get through this together."

Even on a bicycle in the dark, you can feel the good energy. When I first raced Paris-Brest-Paris in 2007, I made the strategic decision to skip sleep on the last night. That meant that I'd be riding at least 24 hours without rest. So, with about 30 miles to go, I was, ah, tired. Riding at a pace that would get me to Paris in just 72 hours, I was ahead of 80% of the riders. But I did have a problem: I was having trouble focusing my eyes. I started seeing shadows running across the dark road where there was nothing to cause them. My leaden legs could barely turn the pedals.

Then I fell in with a pack of crazy Germans who were riding flat out for the finish. We flew through the night, bouncing over cobbles in tiny villages, while their bleary-eyed residents cheered us on. In the wee hours of the morning, the Germans ran stop signs and traffic lights. They zig-zagged through strange towns like they knew the way. I realized that I could either stick with the blitz-krieg or I could fall asleep in a roadside ditch.

> **"Thank you," she said, "for loving me until I could love myself again."**

We blew into the finish about a dozen strong. And they vanished. I don't remember seeing them go. I could not have recognized a single one. So, to my brief Bavarian buddies, all I can say is, "Danke."

## EnergyThink: How Can You Be a Buddy?

Not long ago, I listened to a presentation by a middle-aged woman at Our Daily Bread, the soup kitchen I had helped found decades ago. She once had been a successful businesswoman who had fallen on hard times. Ultimately, she had spiraled down to the streets, losing everything, including her self-respect. But Catholic Charities programs had helped her find her way back out of homelessness and into gainful employment and a place of her own.

"Thank you," she said, "for loving me until I could love myself again."

We may not be homeless, but most of us could use more energy buddies.

⚡ Who are your energy buddies now?

⚡ Whom could you add to your list?

⚡ Energy buddy is a two-way street. To whom could you be a buddy?

⚡ Who needs your help? It could be at work, home, in the community... or beyond.

⚡ What can you offer? Sometimes, it's a talent or a skill. Sometimes, good advice. Sometimes, just an ear to listen or a shoulder to cry on. Often, it can be something you really like to do.

⚡ Like to solve problems? Play golf? Cook? Perform brain surgery? Do income taxes? Fix balky computers? Probably, there's someone who would love to learn from you or benefit from your skills.

⚡ Don't know anybody who needs your help? Lots of non-profits in your community are looking for volunteers.

# 22

# Pumping Emotional Iron

— — — — — — — — — — — — — — —

**"Ah, hard to see, the Dark Side is." —Yoda, Star Wars**

— — — — — — — — — — — — — — —

RACING IN ALASKA IN 2013, I MADE A SERIOUS TACTICAL ERROR IN Fairbanks. The town was the half-way checkpoint in a 750-mile trip from Valdez to Anchorage. Waiting for another rider, I stayed too long and ate too much at lunch. When I rolled out of town, it was hot, hilly and siesta time in the afternoon.

I could barely move. Most of the other riders left me behind. Desperate for a little energy, I stopped at a bar whose name I will never forget, Skinny Dick's Halfway Inn. I downed a Coke, hoping that the sugar and caffeine would revive me. It didn't.

I realized I would have to enlist my two energy buddies, Michael Jackson and Mick Jagger. Pulling out a tiny iPod, I stuck an ear bud in my right ear and cued the rock stars.

Instantly, energy returned. Michael, Mick and I danced up the hills together. I promptly ran down the riders who had escaped. One of them pulled up next to me and said, "Whatever you just did must have been illegal. And I want some of it."

It wasn't illegal, but it was emotional. I usually don't ride with music because, even though I only put the bud in one ear, it makes it harder to hear cars and other riders. But desperate times call for desperate measures. And music works. In fact, the world's best tune for climbing is bagpipes playing "Scotland the Brave." It's no surprise pipers play it in battle.

I learned a music lesson on Kilimanjaro. It took 50 guides and porters to get us 10 Americans to the top. It's cold, dangerous, difficult work. Not only do the porters have to lug their own meager supplies, they have to haul ours, too. So they sing. There is a deep and powerful energy in African music sung by strong young voices. We can find traces of that in blues, soul and rock, but the "real thing" is unmatched.

## Many Paths to Emotional Energy

Music is only one path to more emotional energy. Every time we exercise patience or empathy or confidence, we build emotional energy. Enjoyable, fulfilling activities do the same thing... even if they *look* like a waste of time. It's one of my chief justifications for fishing.

Sometimes, it's better to swap physical energy for emotional energy. For example, one of the prime principles of cycling is aerodynamics. When Lance credits his team for his Tour successes, he is not being falsely modest. A rider tucked behind another rider's rear wheel can use up to 20% less energy. On his successful Tours, Lance almost never came out from behind his energy buddies, shamelessly drafting his way to Yellow Jersey after Yellow Jersey.

> **Every time we exercise patience or empathy or confidence, we build emotional energy.**

So, for many years, I availed myself of the wheels of stronger riders as I, too, shamelessly sucked along in their slipstreams. But now, I sometimes stay at the front for almost an entire ride or race.

Riding "The Big Wild Ride," 750 miles in Alaska, we faced 100 miles of 20-knot-plus headwinds. At times, we were lucky to be going 10 miles an hour. I decided it was easier to lead into the wind and told my buddies to sit on my wheel. Sure, it used more physical energy, but I got two powerful emotional boosts in return. First, I had the satisfaction of helping my friends who were riding with me; second, I got to enjoy the amazing scenery without having to focus on their wheels—or their derrieres. On balance, I went faster, easier with my nose in the wind.[1]

## Marshaling Just Enough Anxiety

A little fear can be emotionally helpful. In his book *Just Enough Anxiety: The Hidden Driver of Business Success*, Robert H. Rosen points out what every sales manager has always known: set a goal that you believe you can reach... barely. (That was my situation on the cross-country ride.) He notes that performance peaks when you have "just enough anxiety." You think you can win the race, hit the sales target, climb the mountain, get an A, lose the weight, earn the promotion, finish the project... but it won't be easy.

Rosen notes that if the goal is too easy, we slack off; if it's too tough, we give up.

Anxiety can be a wonderful spur for creativity, as I often point out in my energy seminars. Oscar Wilde said, "The anxiety is unbearable. I only hope it lasts forever."

## Perfection Can Motivate—Or Waste Energy

For some, the quest for perfection is a great motivator. A technical name for a "perfectionist" is a "maximizer." These folks are driven to make the very best choices. They spend hours researching every purchase. They're constantly looking for a better deal.

Sometimes, being a perfectionist is desirable or even necessary. I want my brain surgeon (if I ever need one) to be a perfectionist. At other times, "perfectionism is slow death," as Hugh Prather said. At the other end of the spectrum is the "satisficer" who believes in "good enough."

To find out which you are, just look at a sample of statements below from Barry Schwartz's book, *The Paradox of Choice: Why More Is Less* (the full test is in the book):[2]

⚡ When faced with choice, I try to imagine all the other possibilities

⚡ No matter how satisfied with my job, I look for better opportunities

⚡ I often check to see if something better is playing on another station

⚡ Relationships are like clothing, try a lot on to find the perfect fit

⚡ I often find it difficult to shop for a gift for a friend

⚡ When renting videos, it's hard to pick the best one.

*—American Psychological Association*

The more you agree with these statements, the more of a maximizer you are. There are no right or wrong answers on this "test." If you're a maximizer, you have to be aware that you might be tempted to waste good energy (and time) trying too hard for the perfect answer. If you're a satisficer, perhaps spending more energy and time on a task might pay dividends.

## EnergyThink: Are You a Maximizer, Satisficer or Somewhere In Between?

Clearly, your status as a maximizer or satisficer depends on the situation. In general, are you a maximizer, a satisficer or somewhere in between?

⚡ What are the implications for your energy and time?

⚡ Anxiety can be your friend... or your foe. Think about what you fear. What's unavoidable? What's necessary? Where could you add or subtract a little anxiety to your benefit? How might you do that?

⚡ One of my favorite New Yorker cartoons depicts two caterpillars regarding a butterfly floating above them. "You'll never get me up in one of those," one caterpillar says to another. What's keeping you from flying?

# 23

# Quitting: The Strategic Choice

---

**"Most ideas are wrong. The best place to be as a scientist is wrong or confused." —Physicist Laurence Krause**

---

"PEOPLE JOIN ORGANIZATIONS; THEY QUIT BOSSES." WHETHER OR NOT that old saw is provably true or not, it certainly is not uncommon. It also makes perfect sense:

⚡ Most new employees know more about the organization than they do about their future boss;

⚡ A "bad" boss can make work hell, even in a great company;

⚡ A change from a "good" boss to a "bad" one can turn a "good" job into a "bad" job.

Notice that I put "good" and "bad" in quotation marks because I define "good" and "bad" in terms of "fit" for you. Often, one person's "bad" boss can be another's "good" boss. Usually, intellectual and emotional energy determines whether a boss is a good fit or not. Often, in my energy seminars, I have this dialog:

*"If your boss represents a major dose of toxic energy for you, should you quit?"* people ask.

Yes. Next question. *"But what about never giving up, never quitting?"*

Short answer: Fuggedaboudit. Long answer: That could very well be one of those "wrong" ideas Laurence Krause is talking about.

*"But what if you don't have anything else lined up? What if you have a family, a dog and a mortgage? What if there are no other jobs? What if..."*

Ben Franklin got it right: "Those who desire to give up freedom to gain security will not have, nor do they deserve, either one."

## Run Toward, Not Away

We're not talking about quitting as in running away; we're talking about quitting as in running *toward*. We're not talking about giving up, we're talking about getting started. Let's say it for all those coaches who told you to "never quit": "Is the halfback running away from the linebacker?" Yes…but the halfback is running *toward* the goal line. *Often, it's advisable to run if you want to score.*

More than four decades ago, Professor Martin Seligman, a psychologist at the University of Pennsylvania, performed a landmark experiment. He put dogs in cages and shocked them until they whimpered and whined in pain. The dogs tried to escape but they couldn't. Eventually, they got used to the pain. Then, Seligman opened the doors to the cages and shocked the dogs again.

They did not leave. From the experiment, he coined the term "learned helplessness."[1] Know anybody whimpering in a cage with an open door?

## Learned Helplessness and PITA: Why Don't You Leave?

At some point, endurance is no longer a virtue. There are many reasons people do not leave "bad" jobs: the money, the security, the lack of other opportunities, the insurance coverage, the commute, golden handcuffs, no better ideas, etc., etc. By now you know the biggest reason: they are afraid to leave.

Many people seek my advice in finding another job or career because I've made successful transitions to different careers in different industries. Often, they say their "bad" boss is the reason they're coming to me. I tell them that a difficult work situation, even though it is a Pain in the Ass (PITA), is actually a blessing. In fact, the more intolerable it is, the better. In a job or life, PITA can also mean:

- ⚡ **P**overty (not just in money);
- ⚡ **I**ntolerable situation;
- ⚡ **T**ermination;
- ⚡ **A**wful boss.

> **A difficult work situation, even though it is a Pain in the Ass, is actually a blessing.**

PITA can be a gift. Why? Remember our friend the Wookie? System One does not like change and System Two is too lazy to do the work to find another job. Frankly, it's the way we're wired. Many will take action only when they see escape as a means of survival. That's too bad because leaving one organization for another is often the only way to grow personally and financially. Gone are the days when you could count on one company to develop, promote and reward you over an entire career.

Yes, it's better if you have another job offer (or a nice cushion of cash to tide you over until you find something else to do). It's always safer to work with a net. But sometimes that's just not possible. Sometimes, your *current* job is taking the time and energy that keeps you from finding a *better* one. All you really need is a direction: something relatively specific that you want to do with your life. "Out" is not a direction... that's running away.

> **Quit when the calculus says that an activity is costing you more than the return on the investment.**

Twice in my career, I have quit jobs with no prospects. Neither time was anxiety-free. Yet they were also two of the most exciting and interesting periods of my life. Ultimately, I discovered new careers that made me much happier than those I had left.

## No Fun... I'm Done

Here's another good reason to quit: it's not fun any more. I'm always amazed by what people do for fun. You may even be wondering that about me (and I don't blame you). Although I have lost friends in bicycle accidents and broken a few bones myself, I look upon the activity as relatively safe.

Yet even though I have a pretty high pain threshold, I ultimately will quit a ride when that seems like the right thing to do. I have to remind myself: THIS IS JUST A BIKE RIDE. I try to put aside the machismo (my friends jokingly call it "Conderaccismo") and pack it in, guilt free. I'm *not* suggesting that you quit when things become unpleasant or difficult. Quit when the calculus says that an activity is costing you more than the return on the investment.

My most notorious example of this was in September 2009, riding The Endless Mountains 750-mile-plus event in central Pennsylvania. Randy Mouri,[2] a good friend, and I were running tied for second about 600 miles in. Hypothermic in a rainstorm, I fell and broke a rib when my shoe jammed in a pedal. I've broken ribs before and the pain wasn't so bad, so I remounted and rode on. Randy was encouraging me to press on since we had endured some of the worst terrain the state had to offer. The accident did decrease my performance a bit though.

However, I began to wonder if I had done internal damage in the fall. In my reduced mental state, I suddenly thought that, if I was really hurt, I would urinate blood. So imagine this: it's the middle of the night in a driving rainstorm. There are two riders standing by the side of the road, lit only by their helmet lights. One is carefully watching the other pee.

I wasn't bleeding. But, after another 20 miles or so, I wised up, quit and went to the hospital to get an X-ray—just to make sure. Looking back, with some sanity restored, I should have quit sooner.

*"I should have quit sooner,"* is also what most of my friends who left unhappy situations say, too.

## EnergyThink: How Can You Broaden Your View?

Positivity guru Barbara Frederickson likes to say, "Negative emotions narrow your range of vision."

Research participants who were in a positive mood were about 50% more likely than those in a negative mood to break out of a rigid mindset, says a team led by Julia S. Haager of the University of Munich in Germany.[3]

So, try broadening your field of vision:

⚡ Often, you don't have to quit to improve your work life. What else could you do and stay on the job?

⚡ Sometimes, you do have to leave to get away from the energy zombies. Hang with the living dead and they will take you with them. What's keeping you from leaving? What are you afraid of? Never getting another job? Depleting all your savings? Living in your car? Is that likely to happen?

In many cases, the risks of staying are actually worse than the risks involved in leaving. Think about it: you're trusting a vampire to keep paying you...

# 24

# The Power of Positive

---

"All mystics…no matter what their theology, no matter what their religion—are unanimous on one thing: that all is well, all is well. Though everything is a mess, all is well. Strange paradox, to be sure. But, tragically, most people never get to see that all is well because they are asleep. They are having a nightmare." —Anthony De Mello, *Awareness*

---

AFTER PSYCHOLOGIST MARTIN SELIGMAN DID HIS FAMOUS EXPERIMENT with the shocked dogs, he realized that most of his profession was devoted to making miserable people less miserable. And—because energy feeds on itself—misery is catching. He tells the now famous story about how his five-year-old daughter complained to him that he was grumpy.

"That girl is the founder of Positive Psychology," he says, half seriously, because her comment awakened in him the realization that the "skills of happiness are not the same as the skills of relieving misery."[1]

Positive Psychology, the new, upbeat wing of the old misery-relieving profession has become increasing popular as more and more people seek to harness the powerful positive emotions in their lives.

One of its more controversial practitioners, Prof. Barbara Frederickson of the University of North Carolina contends that a more positive outlook on life will help you live longer, healthier and happier. In her book *Positivity*, she even offers a test to gauge how positive your outlook is. She asks you to consider 20 questions about the last 24 hours of your life.

## Taking the Automated Positivity Test
Because we all have good days and bad days, Frederickson recommends that you take her test every day for a month and average it. Although

this sounds like a lot of math, you can just go to the website www.positivityratio.com and it will do all the calculations for you, confidentially and for free.

Her contention is that if you can manage a 3/1 ratio of positive emotions to negative emotions—over time—you will flourish. She also says that 80% of the US population is below that level and that 20% have only a 1/1 ratio, which is equivalent to clinical depression. I've found that just taking the test every day improves my outlook on life. It reminds me of all the good stuff that happened over the last day and it also reminds me not to make such a big deal of the negative things. Positive energy fuels more positive energy; energy feeds on itself.

As an extra help, Frederickson also offers her "Positivity Toolkit" which contains great suggestions on how to buff your outlook. The one I like the most is "Build portfolios of positive emotions: joy, gratitude, serenity, interest, hope, pride, amusement, inspiration, awe, love."[2] I have a priest friend who said he keeps a DEATH file in his office. "DEATH" stands for "Damn everything all to hell." On days when he feels like that, he looks in this file which contains many nice mementos. He says it will instantly make him feel better.

> **I have a priest friend who said he keeps a DEATH file in his office. "DEATH" stands for "Damn everything all to hell."**

I realized that I could post on my computer's screen saver many beautiful pictures I had taken on my travels. Now, when my computer "sleeps," it shows scene after scene, awakening many great memories. It's my electronic positive portfolio.

Medical science is just beginning to take seriously the physical benefits of a positive outlook. Hilary Tindle, of the University of Pittsburg School of Medicine, makes a powerful, well documented case (all the way down to the cellular level) in *Up: How Positive Outlook Can Transform Our Health and Aging*. If you think there's no data behind the benefits of optimism, Dr. Tindle will have you thinking again.

## The Power of Positive

One of the most positive guys I know is Bob Brosmer, former Chief Operating Officer of the Y of Central Maryland. The story of Bob's life sounds a lot like the same kind of energy described in this book. In his youth, he and a co-author wrote *Health & High Performance: The Total Approach to Success Through Fitness*, articulating a lot of forward-thinking energy ideas more than 25 years ago.

As a thought-leader at the Y, he advocated many of the concepts in this book and invited me to train their internal leaders on them. He lead the active, high-energy life that makes him a great example for this book. And then, a few months before I wrote this, he suffered a stroke that almost killed him.

Now, he's an even better example. He's using the same energy to re-build his brain. In almost no time, he went from being able to barely lift his arm to being almost completely restored physically. His personality and energy shines clearly through his sudden disability as he strives to restore his language skills.

Suffering from a condition that would depress lesser souls, he instead brightens the day of everybody who visits him. He's one of the energy heroes of this book.

## EnergyThink: What's "No Fish to Clean" for You?

For more than 30 years, my favorite fishing buddy has been Anthony S. Davis, a talented marketer who worked with me both at Catholic Charities and Prudential. Early in our fishing careers, when fish seemed more plentiful, we were both more successful—and more disappointed when we were "skunked." It didn't take us long, though, to discover what every fisherman knows: even a bad day fishing can beat a good day at work. It's about *fishing; not* about catching. When we came home empty-handed, we still came home happy.

"No fish to clean," was Anthony's effort at finding the silver lining in the empty creel. Now, we pretty much practice catch-and-release, returning our fish live to the lake, stream or ocean. "No fish to clean" has become our live-and-let-live mantra. The fish might not understand gratitude, but we are always grateful for the experience.

⚡ What's your version of "no fish to clean"? Do you have to win to be thankful for the chance to play?

⚡ What are the "good things in life" for you? Do they cost a lot of money or take a lot of time and energy? Then why don't you do more of them?

# 25

# Dilbert's Advice: Make Your System *UP*

---

**"To find yourself, think for yourself." —Socrates**

---

THE TIME MANAGEMENT COURSES SAY YOU SHOULD SELECT FOR YOURSELF SMART goals. These Specific-Measurable-Achievable-Realistic-Timely goals are supposed to motivate you. I do believe in goals; really, I do.

But goals have always bothered me because I never got much energy from them. I was never really able to put my finger on the reason... until I read *How to Fail at Almost Everything and Still Win Big, Kind of the Story of My Life*, by Scott Adams. Adams, who created the comic strip *Dilbert*, has this to say about goals: "Goals are for losers."

His argument is that people who live by goals are, at best, in "pre-failure" mode most of the time. Until they reach their goal, they aren't "successful." And, once they do reach their goals, success is fleeting... because they have to move on to a new set of goals. If you're feeling a little unbalanced, perhaps that's because you're on a goals treadmill.

## The Daily Dose of the Dilbert System

What's Adams' alternative to goals? It's *systems*. Here's how he explains it:

> A goal is a specific objective that you either achieve or don't sometime in the future. A system is something you do on a regular basis that increases your odds of happiness in the long run. If you do something every day, it's a system. If you're waiting to achieve it someday in the future, it's a goal.

Adams argues that really successful people use systems, like Warren Buffett's system of investing by buying undervalued companies and holding them indefinitely.

Notice how similar systems are to habits. In a sense, good systems are well-thought-out chains of habits applied consistently (and profitably) over time.

Unlike golf where you know exactly where you are and what the score is, systems can be pretty fuzzy. Before he created Dilbert, Adams decided that his "system" would be to produce something that could be easily reproduced in unlimited quantities and that relied on his creativity. It took him a while to realize it was *Dilbert*.

My broadest "system" is my mission in life: *to use the magic of communication to help people lead happier, more productive, more rewarding lives.* More on life missions later. My business system is to offer extremely short-term training and consulting services (because most other consultants want long-term gigs). My *riding* system is to expend energy wisely over long periods of time. (I let the hot shots sprint up the hills…I'll catch them 100 miles down the road).

> **The annoying thing about goals is that so much of reaching them depends on luck.**

The annoying thing about goals is that so much of reaching them depends on luck—even if it's only the luck of being alive long enough to reach them. When we reach a goal, we're often too eager to pat ourselves on the back, forgetting completely our good fortune. If we fail to reach a goal we're tempted both to blame luck (when it may have been our fault) or to beat ourselves up (when it may have been more a matter of luck). From an energy standpoint, neither is very profitable—or balanced.

The nice thing about systems is that, if you apply your system, you've succeeded in doing that, even though you may have *failed*. I'm in favor of any approach that helps me get beyond my fear of failure so I can learn from it. I like the quote about goals in Christopher McDougall's *Born to Run*, spoken by nuclear engineer and ultra runner Ephraim Romesberg, 65 miles into the Badwater Ultramarathon:

> I always start these events with very lofty goals, like I'm going to do something special And, after a point of body deterioration, the goals get evaluated down to basically where I am now—where the best I can hope for is to avoid throwing up on my shoes.[1]

## EnergyThink: What Are Your Systems?

Goals *are* important. After all, "If you don't know where you're going, you might end up some place else," Yogi Berra famously said. But sometimes, "some place else" can be nice, too. Put aside thinking about goals for a minute and think about your systems.

⚡ What are your "systems"? Unless you think about your routine practices and approaches as systems, you probably move through them unconsciously.

⚡ For example, what's your system for washing clothes, getting to work, or buying holiday presents?

⚡ What's your "system approach" to pleasing your boss, making a sale, or winning an argument (if you ever do) with your significant other?

⚡ Systems often rely on our "stories" and, like stories, you can change your life by changing your systems. Which would you change?

# 26

# Balancing Failure: The Secret of Success

---

**"It is not the critic who counts; not the man who points out how the strong man stumbles, or where the doer of deeds could have done them better. The credit belongs to the man who is actually in the arena, whose face is marred by dust and sweat and blood, who strives valiantly; who errs and comes short again and again; because there is no effort without error and shortcomings; but who does actually strive to do the deed; who knows the great enthusiasm, the great devotion, who spends himself in a worthy cause, who at the best knows in the end the triumph of high achievement and who at the worst, if he fails, at least he fails while daring greatly. So that his place shall never be with those cold and timid souls who know neither victory nor defeat." —Theodore Roosevelt, "Man in the Arena" Speech, April 23, 1910**

---

IN OTHER WORDS, TEDDY SAYS, "DON'T LET FAILURE THROW YOU OFF balance."

One of my toughest challenges as a teacher is persuading my students to fail well. Most of us hate to fail and expect (and often get) punishment for it. Again, the academic system is notorious for punishing students for failure, completely missing the learning opportunity embedded within it.

The discipline (if you can call it that) I teach is marketing. My students are the universally gifted and diverse cohort that regularly passes through the Johns Hopkins Bloomberg School of Public Health. Because Bloomberg is perennially rated Number One in the nation (if not the world), it gets the cream of the crop. Some of my students are already MDs and PhDs.

Most have never taken a marketing course before.

Now, if I was teaching golf to people who had never golfed before, few, if any, of them would expect to break 100 on their first 18 holes. Putting aside the indisputable fact that marketing is easier than golf, the students still expect A's. This raises the deep philosophical question of what they should get an A *for*.

- ⚡ For doing brilliant work? Most of them will not do that. They don't have the experience or the training.

- ⚡ For effort? Some of the biggest failures in the history of marketing have stemmed from trying too hard.

- ⚡ For showing up? The trend in academia toward grade inflation would support this, but it leaves a funny taste in my mouth.

- ⚡ For "failing while daring greatly"? Yes! Because if there is any lesson to be learned in a marketing class it is that successful campaigns are the often-accidental product of many failures.

So I intentionally do not give them too much information for assignments. I want them to use their imagination. I especially don't want them to think that there is only one way to "do it right." This is no math class. And I certainly don't want them to be afraid to fail.

"It's okay to fail," I tell them. "I want you to try hard... have fun... and then fail. It's the best way to learn. It's much better to fail here, in school where it doesn't 'count,' than out there in the real world, where it *does*."

> **I certainly don't want them to be afraid to fail.**

One of the most refreshing aspects of my favorite cycling sport, Randonneuring, is that it is a race... and it's not. Like any other race, your time is recorded. But you don't get anything special for winning beyond the satisfaction of completing the ride. I've "won" a few, finished well in others and didn't finish at all in a couple. I learned the most in the last category and almost nothing from winning.

## Failure is Your Friend?

Once, I had a very creative musician friend whose car license plate featured a single word: FAILURE. When I asked him about driving around with such a negative message, he responded, "Negative? Everything I've ever learned I learned from failure."

"You gotta be willing to fail," said Apple CEO Steve Jobs in a famous 1994 interview.[1] "You gotta be willing to crash and burn... If you're afraid of failing you won't get very far."

The problem with winning is that you tend not to change. If it's not broken, why fix it? The world changes fast and what worked yesterday won't work tomorrow. Monte Burke, the *Forbes* staff writer and the fishing guide on the Weather Channel said it perfectly:

> Don't fish yesterday's fish. Just because you were successful doing something yesterday, or if one tactic worked for a week, or a month, or a year, that was then. You have to figure out the now. Tides change, weather changes, fish move. Try to look ahead to the next spot, where you can use the knowledge you gained at your old spot. That's how you repeat success.

In the 1994 World Cup final, Italy and Brazil fought to a 0-0 tie and then went on to settle the match with penalty kicks. Roberto Baggio, one of the world's premier soccer players, sent his kick sailing over the head of the goal, losing the game for Italy. In his biography, he says simply that it was the worst moment of his career. He confesses that the pain of that instant failure affected him for years and still haunts his dreams. Yet his ultimate insight is most powerful:

"Only those who have the courage to take a penalty (shot) miss them."

## EnergyThink: How Will You Fail... Wonderfully?

"The tiny cost of failure," wrote marketing guru Seth Godin in his November 7, 2014 blog, "is dwarfed by the huge cost of not trying."

⚡ Nobody *likes* to fail. It's that System One "Wookie" part of our brain that doesn't want to lose. What can you do to accept the fact that everybody, including you, does? That might make failure more tolerable.

⚡ How does fear of failure get in your way? Does it keep you from growing? From trying new experiences? From meeting new people?

⚡ How do *you* get beyond the fear of failure?

# PART SIX

# Tapping Spiritual Energy

# 27

# The Mystery of Spiritual *UP*

---

**"Positive emotion alienated from the exercise of
character leads to emptiness, to inauthenticity, to
depression, and, as we age, to the gnawing realization
that we are fidgeting until we die." —Martin Seligman**

---

SPIRITUAL ENERGY IS MISSION-DRIVEN; IT'S ALL ABOUT YOUR IDENTITY
and values.

The most intangible and elusive energy reservoir of them all, spiritual
energy fuels passion, commitment and endurance. Although for many it
is religious in nature, it does not have to be. Frequently, powerful people
we admire have it. It's indispensable for great leaders and also for great
mothers and fathers, great kids, great friends, great lovers and great heroes of all kinds. To me, spiritual energy is embedded in each person's
*mission*, his or her life's purpose.

## Frank's Long Walk

Before we go too far into spiritual energy, there is Frank Ryan's story. The
retired Marine colonel and Certified Public Accountant is the board chair
of The Good Shepherd Center. The Baltimore center, run by the Sisters
of the Good Shepherd, cares for severely emotionally-disturbed girls and
boys. It is extremely difficult, risky work.

Kind of like being a Marine, but without the gunfire.

So it's no surprise that Frank has been on the board of the center for
decades. In 2014, he undertook a fundraising scheme that captured the
imagination (and the money) of many and the skepticism of quite a few: he
would walk across the country telling the Good Shepherd story. No small

feat for a younger person, but Frank was 62, an age where many would find it hard to walk 18 holes of golf.

His successful coast-to-coast march took him 2,800 miles across deserts, up and down mountains, and through endless farmland. Heat, hunger, wind, cold and rain could not stop him, even though it took him over 150 days, about 50 more than he had expected. He limped through the long days with bleeding feet, aching joints and a crippling muscle injury so he could help the nuns and their dedicated staff bring a better life to their kids.

> **Heat, hunger, wind, cold and rain could not stop him, even though it took him over 150 days.**

In his book, *Life Lessons Learned: Amazing Stories of My Walk Across America for Children*, the most amazing stories aren't about what happened to him externally. They are about his deep faith and incredible perseverance. Frank calls the mega-hike his "Walk of Atonement and Gratitude," an effort to rebalance what he did wrong in his life with a great big RIGHT—and to be thankful for the opportunity to do it.

"My plan was to ask every person I have hurt to forgive me, every person that I have disappointed to pray for me, and every person that I helped to help another," he says simply.

His most touching story involved meeting a homeless man who gave Frank all the money in his tattered pocket: $10.40. "I abused my daughter," the homeless man confessed. Frank turned over the small gift at the center's 150th anniversary celebration. There wasn't a dry eye—including Frank's—in the place.

Frank may no longer be an active Marine, but he is still very much true to the Corps' motto: *Semper Fidelis*, "Always Faithful." It's a motto that has motivated many to sacrifice their lives. It captures the character and values of both the branch and its men and women.

## Frank and His Miraculous Rosary

Every day, as Frank walked across the country, I sent him a short email with a bit of inspiration I scrounged from a variety of sources. It was a little thing that any good energy buddy would do. In his book, he claims that he would never have made it across the country without my small doses of encouragement. Knowing Frank, I have no doubt he would have made it without me—even if the fires of hell stood in the way.

When I rode across the country, Frank returned the favor. Every day, he would send me an email, telling me that he was praying for me. One evening before an especially difficult day, I sent him a note that I was anticipating the most challenging climbing of the entire trip. He responded that he had prayed a rosary for me.

I awoke to gale force winds and driving rain.

"So much for the rosary," I thought.

But then ride boss Lon Haldeman announced that, because of the threatening weather (that, incidentally, included a tornado or two), we were going to change routes. Instead of criss-crossing a brutal ridge, we were going to ride right down the valley: almost no steep climbing.

An auspicious start, but the gale raged on. Although it was after sunrise, it was dark as night as we rolled out, buffeted by savage winds. Leaning into the storm, I had to wrestle the machine to keep it on the road. Even the cars were crawling over the flooded pavement, dowsing us with every pass. It made little difference; we couldn't be more wet. I threaded my way through a submerged minefield of roadside debris: rocks, cracks, potholes, bottles and shredded truck tires.

> **At the edge of the road and the edge of my mind, the voice of fear began to whisper.**

At the edge of the road and the edge of my mind, the voice of fear began to whisper: "This is miserable. This is dangerous. You could be blown off the road or into a truck. These downhill runs are twisty and slick. Your tires won't hold."

I thought about Frank and his rosary and started to recite the old "Ave Maria" prayer to the rhythm of my pedaling:

Hail Mary, full of grace, the Lord is with thee.
Blessed art thou amongst women
And blessed is the Fruit of thy Womb, Jesus.
Holy Mary, Mother of God,
Pray for us sinners now
And at the hour of our death. Amen.

Sloshing along, repeating the ancient prayer over and over again through gritted teeth, I began to regain my composure. The sound of the words mingled with the swish of the tires and the rasp of a grime-soaked chain. I retreated deep inside my flapping rain jacket, searching for warmth and peace amid the cold fury of the storm.

In a couple of hours, the storm subsided and the road drained. After a very damp start, we rode dry and fast all day. Was it the rosary? I know what Frank would say.[1]

## Ask Lance: Spiritual Energy Isn't Always "Good"

Don't make the mistake of thinking that all spiritual energy is good. The passion, commitment and endurance that kept Lance Armstrong cheating, lying for years about it, and suing people who accused him of it was "spiritual," too. The world is full of "mean spirited" people who act selfishly, take pleasure in others' suffering and often cause it.

Whether or not you believe in Satan, Lucifer or evil spirits, you probably know people who at least metaphorically made a "deal with the devil" by "selling their soul" for apparent gain: wealth, fame, power, or whatever.

Under any dangerous movement (good or bad), there is usually a strong spiritual base. Clearly, the terrorists who attacked the World Trade Center had lots of spiritual energy. Think of spiritual energy in terms of its potential positive and negative characteristics. You can imagine a graph like the one below (see illustration #4), with positive energy on the Y axis and negative on the X. "Zero" is complete apathy; at the top of the Y is total unselfish love; at the end of the X is utter hate.

> **Under any dangerous movement (good or bad), there is usually a strong spiritual base.**

It doesn't take much to see Gandhi and other heroes at the pinnacle of Y and Hitler, Stalin and other scoundrels on tail of X. You'll notice that they all changed the world pretty dramatically. I like to think I'm way down the Y, but struggling upward, rather imperfectly. Where are you?

## Spiritual Sinks: What's Your Life Worth?

"I used to care, but I took a pill for that," reads the inscription on a popular T-shirt. The shirt captures the exact opposite sentiment of *Semper Fi*. It's the perfect diagnosis of spiritual death.

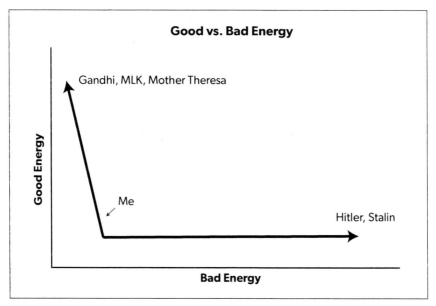

*Illustration #4: All energy is not "good" energy. Where do you see yourself?*

The spiritual sinks are all too common: lack of motivation and commitment, no sense of direction, no deep purpose. In a materialistic world, the extrinsic motivators of money, fame, power, toys, fun and the like can swamp the intrinsic motivators that grow from values deep inside.

"Is the life you're living worth what you're giving up to have it?" I ask my audiences across the country. Frequently, the answer is "no," although few will say it out loud. Occasionally, people will come up to me after a talk and say flatly, "I have no purpose in my life."

More frequently, I can see it in their eyes. Or I can feel it in the distracted, detached way they behave.

*I do have a T-shirt slogan that I much prefer: "Find something you would die for—and live for it."*

## EnergyThink: What Does Spiritual Energy Mean to You?

Once, when I was visiting Baltimore Catholic Charities Gallagher Services, which serves developmentally disabled adults, I had a conversation with the spiritual director. A Protestant minister and a woman, she demonstrated that ecumenism was alive and well—at least in this one Catholic program.

"Is it difficult to work with disabled adults?" I asked her. She looked at me quizzically and responded, "Well, they're not retarded *spiritually,* you know."

It got me to thinking how often we conflate the spiritual and the intellectual, probably because we so often over-think our spirituality. Spirituality is not the same as theology. We also sometimes confuse spirituality with the emotional "feelings" around religious holidays like Passover and Christmas. It's not wrong; we're human and we contain physical, emotional, intellectual and spiritual energy all at once. My argument here, though, is that it pays to identify those elements deep inside that give us spiritual strength. If energy feeds on energy, the biggest supply is spiritual.

What is the manifestation of spiritual energy for you? Is it:

⚡ What you would die for? Family members, the nation, peace, freedom or some other cause?

⚡ What you would live for? Your identity; the things you love to do? What you believe you *must* do?

⚡ Your core beliefs? Your faith? Your principles?

⚡ Where do you see yourself on the Love-Apathy-Hate graph?

# 28

## Confronting the Challenge
## of Calvin...and Cancer

---

**"If you're going through hell, keep
going." —Winston Churchill**

---

JOHN FUOCO SAT ON THE EDGE OF THE BED, LOOKING GRAY, GRAVE
and in pain. As the strictures in his bowels blocked the beans and rice he
had shared with me a few hours earlier, I waited for his signal to call 911.

He wasn't supposed to be here. He was supposed to be in a hospital
bed recovering from the operation that he had postponed so that he could
race his bicycle.

"Good thing he's a doctor," I thought. "He must know what he's doing."
But then I remembered that a blown intestine doesn't much care what
your degree is.

Then the pain passed and he relaxed. We'd be racing in the morning.

The fact that John was even alive, much less racing in a national event,
was nothing short of a miracle. In particular it is a miracle built on the
personal character and courage that comes from a wealth of spiritual
energy. In 2011, as most of us were preparing for Paris-Brest-Paris, we got
a note from John's spouse that he would not be going. At first, this was
puzzling, since he had done really well four years earlier.

Later, we learned John had lung cancer. A world-class long-distance
bike racer who never smoked, he would be the last person one would
suspect for this deadly disease. Nonetheless, it was cancer and it was
serious. The doctors removed half of one lung. "Think of it like a shark
bite," John would say later. It would take him days to even bring himself
to look at the scar.

Then they put him on chemotherapy so severe that half the patients who try it either give up the treatment and choose death—or die while on the treatment.

## "The First Treatment Was the Worst"

"The very first treatment was the worst," he would write later. "Despite being in the medical field and being told about the effects of my particular chemo drugs I was just not prepared for what they did. Nausea does not describe the nausea. Sick does not describe the sick. It was a half metallic, poisoned sensation that crept immediately to the tips of my fingers and toes and into my saliva as the drugs were infused. For the couple of days after each treatment I had that poisoned taste and feeling.

"I tried going for short walks with varying success. Once I had to phone my wife to pick me up two blocks from the house. I could not take one more step and would have been embarrassed to have the neighbors see me lying on the side of the road. I cried, out of desperation, in the shower after that, just not believing I could endure three more months of this."

Suddenly, the rider who once could fly up hills was struggling to climb a short flight of steps. In one of our email exchanges, he told me to hold the following May 4. We would be racing Calvin's Challenge, a 12-hour endurance event in Ohio that he once had dominated.

## Spiritually *UP*: A Guy Named "Fire"

I put the date on my calendar, but I didn't register for the event. I underestimated the spiritual strength of John Fuoco. In Italian, "fuoco" means fire. John's passion for riding burned brighter than his cancer. Being a bike rider was an important part of his identity and cancer was not going to change that.

As soon as he could, John got back on the bike. Before long, he was logging serious miles. Not as fast as he once was, but just as determined. He, Andrea, and I did a test ride at 300 kilometers and he powered through. He was ready. He was a great living example of William James' words:

Beyond the very extreme of fatigue and distress, we may find amounts of ease and power we never dreamed ourselves to own; sources of strength never taxed at all because we never push through the obstruction.

But just as John's energy was heating up, seeming disaster struck again. Scar tissue from his earlier operation was strangling his guts. He needed another operation as soon as possible, his doctors said. But they didn't know John. A mere life-threatening situation was hardly enough to change his mind. Besides, a week after the race, his daughter was graduating from college and he wasn't going to miss that either.

So on the morning of May 4, 2012, only a year after a major operation and a few months after chemotherapy, John, Andrea and I stood on the starting line at Calvin's Challenge. The race would test our mettle...in unexpected ways.

> **A mere life-threatening situation was hardly enough to change his mind.**

Calvin's is a unique event. It's a free-for-all, with riders jockeying in fast packs to see how far they can go in 12 hours. The easy, rolling countryside around Springfield, Ohio is ideal for speed.

And speed we did. At seven-and-a-half hours, we had ridden 150 miles, a pace probably good enough for each of us to medal in our age classes. As we wheeled into the pits to replenish food and water, we noticed that Andrea was looking ashen.

"You go on without me," she said. The pace and the pressure had caught up with her stomach. She couldn't hold anything down and she had weakened significantly. I turned to John, for whom this could very well be his last race. Besides the strictures in his bowels, the cancer had returned. He might never turn a pedal in competition again. This might be his last chance.

He didn't hesitate for a moment. He wasn't going to leave her. "Let's pedal easy," he said. "She might recover."

## Winning the Blood Pressure Bet

She never did. But she didn't quit, either. Our pace halved as she soldiered along. We went from ahead to behind, with the ominous "broom wagon" tracking us as we clicked off the final miles. At one point, concerned that dehydration might cause Andrea to pass out on the bike, John stopped the following truck to borrow a stethoscope and a blood pressure cuff. He and I placed bets on her blood pressure. If it was too low, we agreed to quit. He guessed low. I guessed her blood pressure almost perfectly; she was good to go on.

We logged 200 miles, just enough for Andrea to win her first racing medal but out of the money for John and me. John couldn't have been more proud and happy if he had just won the Tour de France. He had placed his personal racing success behind him in exchange for a much richer reward.

"I don't know what the future holds for me, but if my cycling life is to be at an end, I've crowned it with one last joyous achievement," he wrote after the race. "And with that I feel satisfied."

## EnergyThink: What's Your Spiritual Energy Story?

I happen to think that John's cancer story, which is an ongoing struggle between his identity and his disease, is beyond inspiring. It's not about winning; it's about persevering no matter what. In 2015, while he was on chemo fighting cancer, John rode his bike 5,000 miles. His story certainly isn't about dying...it's about living.

Our battles rage every day:

⚡ What has tested your spiritual mettle?

⚡ When did you find the strength to "do the right thing" even though it was difficult to do so?

⚡ When were you able to "keep on keeping on" despite pain, sorrow, exhaustion, discouragement, depression, etc.?

⚡ What did you learn from the experience? Can you draw on that strength now? Do you?

⚡ Someone once said, "It's better to be kind than right." What has your experience been?

# 29

# Spiritual Energy Links to Your Mission

---

*"I want to give like I have plenty
I want to love like I'm not afraid
I want to be the one I was meant to be
I want to be the way I was made."*
**—Chris Tomlin, "The Way I Was Made"**

---

ONE KEY TO SPIRITUAL ENERGY IS YOUR "MISSION" OR PURPOSE. JOHN Fuoco can cycle through cancer because, deep inside, he's not just a physician—he's a *rider* and a very special human being. We're all special in our own ways; a mission is a powerful way to explain that—to ourselves and the rest of the world.

In my seminars, I have helped many hundreds of people articulate their life's mission, and in the next chapter, I will tell you how I do it (and how you can, too).

By mission, I mean the "reason you are on earth." I don't mean "goal." Goals are great, and you'll be more likely to reach your goals (and understand why you want to reach them), if you're living your mission. Goals sound like "I want to be a good parent" and "I want to retire early with more toys" and "I want to get to heaven" and "I want a promotion." These are all fine goals, but they are *not* missions.

Missions are all about what you DO. I mean this in the broadest, most inclusive sense. So, for example, a Labrador Retriever fetches. Hawks hunt. Peach trees provide fruit. Everything in nature serves a purpose, indeed, many purposes. Mother Nature has woven everything together in a marvelous ecology. It's one reason that we fear losing an animal or plant to extinction. Another piece of the natural tapestry will be missing and we're not always sure how it fits. If we cut down all the oaks, the squirrels will starve. If we wipe out the ozone layer, we all will fry.

People are infinitely more complex than retrievers or hawks. We all do many things. Yet there is *something* in each of us that says "*This* is what you do." Finding that is the key to discovering the source of your spiritual energy.

## Why Are You Here?

When there weren't many women on Capitol Hill, Rep. Clare Boothe Luce challenged John F. Kennedy: "A great man is one sentence. What is your sentence?" This is what we're looking for: a word, a sentence, an idea, a metaphor or an image that answers the question, "Why am I here?" It's an integral part of your identity and a source of great energy. "The soul cannot live without purpose and meaning," says Richard Rohr, Franciscan priest and lecturer.

A mission is like a compass. It gives you your bearings. Knowing where north is helps—even when you're not heading north.

> **"The soul cannot live without purpose and meaning."**

I do a lot of identity work with organizations and teams. Central to determining a company's brand is its mission. Powerful missions often drive success. When I take organizations or groups through a branding process, I begin with the personal missions of each of the people in the room. Whether they are an executive team, project team, or a board of directors, they will most quickly and effectively reach their joint mission by understanding their individual ones.

## Mother Nature is Not Stupid

Although finding your mission sounds philosophical or even theological, it often helps just to think of it like branding. Indeed, all you have to believe to do the process is that *Mother Nature is not stupid.* That assumption seems to work for almost everybody because, whether or not you believe in God, the Force, the Cosmos, or nothing, you gotta hand it to Mother Nature. She's kept things together pretty well for a few billion years and she's likely to keep on keeping on for a while.

Let's look at our doggy friend, the Lab. Like every living thing, retrievers have a purpose. As I said earlier, Labs fetch. Mother Nature, with a little help from breeders, has endowed Labs with the talents they need to fetch. Also, not being stupid, she gave them an incentive to use their talents in line with their mission. When they are fetching, they get a big shot of dopamine (which is a brain chemical that acts just like it sounds). They *LOVE* to fetch. Just ask any Lab owner how long he or she can throw that ball before the Lab wants to stop.

It's the same for us. When we are doing our mission, we are thoroughly enjoying ourselves, often at a very deep, profound level. Which is part of Mother Nature's plan. We love to do what we do, so we do it and we get better at it. It's a little bit of evolution in each of our lives. Or, as Father Rohr says, "Your image of God creates you."[1]

## EnergyThink: What's Mother Nature's "Secret" for You?

Ralph Waldo Emerson said, "One look at the face of heaven and earth lays all petulance at rest, and soothes us to wiser convictions. To the intelligent, nature converts itself into a vast promise, and will not be rashly explained. Her secret is untold."

⚡ What's Mother Nature's "secret" purpose when it comes to you?

⚡ What have been her "hints"? What activities give you pleasure and make you happy?

# 30

# What You Do: Creating Your Mission Vocabulary

"Work like you don't need the money. Love like you've never been hurt. Dance like nobody's watching." —Pitcher Satchel Paige

IF YOU'RE GOING TO WRITE YOUR MISSION, YOU'LL NEED A VOCABU-lary. In this chapter, you'll build one for yourself. Understand that you are doing a *draft* mission. It will be quick and dirty. You have the rest of your life to polish it.

Usually, when I am working with a group, the entire mission process takes only a couple hours. That time includes sharing everyone's vocabulary. Often, missions done in a group are better because people get ideas from each other. Unlike school, in this process it's perfectly all right to copy from anybody.

I'm going to assume that you're doing this alone, but feel free to do it with friends. It's a great exercise to bring together a team or to even introduce a number of strangers to each other. It's the fastest way I know to learn a lot about someone else.

> It's the fastest way I know to learn a lot about someone else.

Some people are concerned that, in writing their missions, they'll betray some secret about themselves. Not very likely. You've been living your mission all your life and everybody who knows you knows what it is. It's as public as your face. You just haven't *articulated* it yet because, well, when you're in the frame, it's hard to see the picture.

## Verbs: What You Do

A mission is about what you *do*. In third grade, we learned that "do" words were called "verbs." So, just make a list of verbs that describe what you do. Here's how it works:

⚡ Include especially words that describe what you like to do. Remember, Mother Nature wants you to enjoy your mission. If you ski once a year, but you love it, "ski" is a good verb for you.

⚡ Include both "at work" and "evening and weekend" verbs. Gandhi said, "My life is an indivisible whole, and all my activities run into one another…. My life is my message." All the words are good for your mission.

⚡ Don't spend a lot of time thinking about the words, just let them flow, one after another, down the page. Don't worry about "purpose" with a capital "P" at this point.

⚡ Don't bother including verbs that are common to everybody. "Eat, think, sleep, walk, talk, drive, work" don't get you much traction. On the other hand, "think about nuclear fusion," "drive a Formula One race car," and "work on the perfect martini" are very differentiating. As you can see, "verbs" can also be phrases.

The "verb list" is the most important list. It can be enormously revealing. Not only does the content of the list say volumes about you, but the order of the words can reveal how you think. Finally, the amount of energy attached to the saying of the words is powerful. Often, in a room of complete strangers, people can easily identify the words that give you the most energy. Pretend that your pen or pencil is a Geiger counter and run it down the page. Which words register the most energy?

Go through and "unpack" words that have a lot of meaning for you. For example, if you wrote down "help people at work," think about how you do that. Do you "explain… challenge… question… support… lead… coach… mentor… listen"? Each and every one of those is better than just "help."

## Values: *Why* You Do It

Next, make a list of your values. Values, if they are the real thing and not just a list of platitudes, are powerful because they explain to you and others how you run your life. They are the way you make decisions. The same goes for organizations. When I visit companies and ask the employees what the company values are, I usually get blank looks. Sometimes, that's a clear indication that the "values page" on the company website is just another page on the website.

Sometimes, though, people don't articulate their values because they are completely internalized. Usually, you can tell pretty quickly how serious people are about their values. For example, the Enron code of ethics said, "Relations with the company's many publics—customers, stockholders, governments, employees, suppliers, press and bankers—will be conducted in honesty, candor and fairness." Its CEO, Kenneth Lay, is famous for saying, "Rules are important, but you should not be a slave to rules, either."[1]

> **Just ask, "So how do you spend your time and your money?"**

There's an easy way to cut through the bull for people. After you get the list of values, just ask, "So how do you spend your time and your money?"

Therefore, on the values list, include what you value. These can be the "Capital V" values like "Honesty and Integrity" (the two favorites), The Golden Rule, The Ten Commandments, and the Boy Scout Oath and the Girl Scout Promise. But don't stop there. Also include what I call "preferences" like chocolate, single malt scotch, long walks on the beach, fly fishing, taking advantage of a great sale, clean air, vacations, etc.

Don't bother separating the two sets, just let them flow.

## VIPs: Why You Do It For *Them*

Then, make a list of your Very Important Persons. For many people, this is the hardest list. It's not because it's hard to imagine who's important; it's because they are *two* types of VIPs. The first type are friends, family, colleagues and customers. You can put them all down, of course. But I usually tell folks just to say those four words—friends, family, colleagues, customers—and then focus on the *other* list.

The "other" list can include some of the same people, but you should describe them differently. This list includes *people who, when they come to you for help, you **want** to help them.* Think about all the people who have come to you for help over the course of your life. Some were an annoyance. Some, though, you delighted in helping; you said "yes" because you *wanted* to help. Just like the Lab who will dive happily into the frigid lake to retrieve a bird.

Often, this list is short, but revealing. These people *knew* what your mission was. Do you always get asked to organize the church picnic? Do you enjoy fixing others' broken cars? Do people always ask you to decipher complicated problems? Is everybody always sharing problems with you because you listen?

These VIPs can be the elderly, children, the confused, the technically challenged, the afraid, the tired, the worried, the handicapped, the homeless, the sick, the injured, the underdogs, the confused, the overweight, the discouraged. Here's a common list that I hear. People who:

⚡ Are hurting

⚡ Want to help themselves

⚡ Have great potential

⚡ Have little potential

⚡ Face tough decisions

⚡ Want to make the world better

⚡ Are talented

⚡ Are baffled by technology

⚡ Want to learn an activity or sport

⚡ Are working for clean air and water

⚡ Are in my company or favorite charity.

Sometimes this list even includes non-people. In some of my courses, people have mentioned specific breeds of cats, dogs and horses. Some folks have even mentioned the Spotted Owl and the Everglades.

## EnergyThink: Can You Expand Your Mission Vocabulary?

Marketing Guru Seth Godin famously asked, "What if surfing was your job? Same waves, different day."

"Where would you go on vacation?" he asked. "Your drudgery is another person's delight. It's only a job if you treat it that way. The privilege to do our work, to be in control of the promises we make and the things we build, is something worth cherishing."[2]

⚡ What do you *do*...really?

⚡ Are you in control of the promises you make and the things you build?

⚡ If not, what would you do if you *were* in control?

⚡ What's keeping you from that?

# 31

# Flipping the Identity Switch:
# Your Mission

---

**"The goal of the hero's journey is yourself,
finding yourself." —Joseph Campbell**

---

LONG, LONG AGO, IN AN AMERICA VERY DIFFERENT FROM TODAY'S, there was a "Space Race." The U.S. was locked in a Cold War with the Russians and the focus was on the "Last Frontier" and carrying our supremacy into space. The most visible warriors in this struggle were the astronauts.

One of the early astronauts, L. Gordon Cooper, in the book *We Seven*, wrote years later of the rigorous tests to determine whether a candidate indeed possessed the "Right Stuff." The "Right Stuff" meant the skills, character and courage to step into the unknown and dangerous worlds of space—and global public relations.

Because the eyes of the world would be focused on these heroes, their personal identity was critical. In addition to riding rocket sleds and experiencing weightlessness in diving planes, each man was given a blank pad and a pencil and ordered to complete the sentence "I am..." as many times as possible. Cooper said it was one of the most challenging tests.

And that's where you are now.

Remember that your mission is *not* a secret. You've been living your mission all your life. Ideally, when you articulate it for a friend or relative, they should say "Well, *everybody knows that* about you."

If you've created the three vocabularies in the last chapter, you probably have in front of you all the information you need. You don't *have* to use any of those words, but the chances are good that the ideas are all there.

Some folks merely pick a verb, a value and a VIP and say something like "I do *this* because of *this* for *these people*."

That's fine, but often a more powerful approach is to use a metaphor or an image that not only captures what you do physically, but intellectually, emotionally and spiritually as well.

## What's a Mission Like?

The short answer is that it's like *you*.

All of my marketing students have to go through the exercise to help them understand branding. One was struggling with his mission when suddenly he announced, "I am the doorman at the party of life!" Everyone laughed, but he did want to go on to pursue a career in entertainment or hospitality. To him, it wasn't a joke.

> **"I am the doorman at the party of life!"**

Many years ago, I worked with young lady with the classic problem: "I don't know what I want to do with the rest of my life." Her favorite verb was "**shop**," so she thought she might become a buyer at a department store. But one of her values was to "live in New York City." Buyers don't make much money and she would have had to struggle in Manhattan.

She "unpacked" the word "shop." What she really meant was "helping people find good fits." She would have been just as happy shopping for a tie to match my suit as she would have been to buy a dress for herself. "**Finding good fits**" was a powerful mission. She became a successful executive recruiter (finding the right person for a job) and then went into commercial real estate (finding the right building for a company).

## What Do You Do For Fun?

Often, what people do for fun can be very revealing. That's because we often have more control over that than a job choice. "We are at home in our games because it is the only place we know just what we are supposed to do," Albert Camus once said. We like the clear rules, clear purpose, and clear goals of recreational activities; they are so much less messy than "life." It's one of the pleasures of running ultramarathons, says Dean Karnazes who routinely runs night and day…for days.[1]

Once a financial executive told me his verb was "**surf**." As a youth, he surfed all over the world. But when he "grew up," he discovered trading stocks. In surfing, the point is choosing the right wave, knowing when to get on and knowing when to get off. In his job as a trader, the point is choosing the right stock and knowing when to buy and when to sell. After years in the water, he felt right at home on the high-adrenalin environment of the trading desk. "It's the same thing," he said. "I love my job."

Speaking of water, a salesman who was a SCUBA diver told me that the favorite part of his hobby was taking people down for the first time. "It's a whole new world down there," he said excitedly. What did he enjoy most about his job? "I help people discover new ideas... **I help them get their feet wet.**"

Once, a half-marathoner described her mission as "**mile eleven**"— helping people finish what they started, even when they may be tired and discouraged (just like half marathoners feel toward the end of the race). A CPA once told me she was a "**jump partner**," the person to which novice parachutists strap themselves. That way, they can make the jump without

> **"I help people discover new ideas... I help them get their feet wet."**

having to worry about opening the parachute. With her, her clients can take the important steps they need to take... with less worry.

Sometimes, a single word is all it takes. I know many "**bartenders**" who never serve a drink ("they listen and make people feel better") and "**gardeners**" who never get their hands dirty ("they make things grow") and "**guides**" ("they show people the way"). Once I was working with a man who said he was a "**coach**."

"What kind of coach are you?" I asked.

"I'm a **second half coach**," he replied. "When you're in the state championship and you're two touchdowns behind and your quarterback has broken his leg and your game plan is not working and the fans are booing, that's when you want me."

I tell folks that I am a "**word wizard**." *I use the magic of communication to help people live happier, more productive and more rewarding lives.*

## Many More Missions—To Prime Your Pump

Here are some of the more interesting missions out of the hundreds I have heard over many years. These examples are here to prime your pump; don't just pick one and go with it:

- ⚡ Acorn guy
- ⚡ Air traffic controller
- ⚡ Big comfy couch
- ⚡ Black diamond challenger
- ⚡ Border Collie
- ⚡ Bridge builder
- ⚡ Caddy
- ⚡ Camp director
- ⚡ Caretaker
- ⚡ Catalyst
- ⚡ Chain link
- ⚡ Cheerleader
- ⚡ Chess coach
- ⚡ Chess player
- ⚡ Collaborative creator
- ⚡ Compassionate advocate
- ⚡ Connect through conflict
- ⚡ Constant tinkerer
- ⚡ Creative cake baker
- ⚡ Cruise director
- ⚡ Crutch
- ⚡ Doctor Feelgood
- ⚡ Dot connector
- ⚡ Dragon slayer
- ⚡ Duct tape

⚡ Enabler

⚡ Engendering trust in technology

⚡ Explorer of possibilities

⚡ Field general

⚡ Find common ground

⚡ First aid

⚡ Fishing instructor

⚡ Forest ranger

⚡ Fortune teller

⚡ Freedom to reach your potential

⚡ Game show host

⚡ GPS

⚡ Grease

⚡ Guide dog

⚡ Hammer

⚡ Handyman

⚡ Help people find more freedom

⚡ Help people realize their dreams

⚡ Hunter-gatherer

⚡ Ice breaker

⚡ Integrator

⚡ Juggler with style

⚡ Kitchen sponge

⚡ Last arrow in the quiver

⚡ Last man standing

⚡ Life whisperer

⚡ Lifeline

⚡ Light switch

⚡ Lioness

⚡ Look under the rock

⚡ Magellan

⚡ Marathon coach

⚡ Mr. Odd Jobs

⚡ Navigator

⚡ Non-status-quo-er

⚡ Nurturer

⚡ Oracle

⚡ Origami

⚡ Pain reliever

⚡ Pathfinder

⚡ Pit bull

⚡ Plays nice with others

⚡ Point guard

⚡ Prepare independent people for change

⚡ Progressive referee

⚡ Purposeful pollinator

⚡ Puzzle solver

⚡ Quarterback

⚡ Ray of sunshine

⚡ Re-arranger of deck chairs

- Rommel
- Safe harbor
- Scout master
- Scrap-booker
- Sherpa
- Ship pilot
- Shoe salesman
- Smokey the Bear
- Social proctologist
- Solving life's puzzles
- Sound engineer
- Story teller
- Strategic hand holder
- Strategizer-Connector-Worrier-Synthesizer
- Stress-buster
- Swimmer with sharks
- Symphony conductor
- Tailor/mender
- Thinking man's self-help book
- Toymaker
- Tumble weed
- Waiter
- War-time consigliore
- Watering can
- Weed and feed

⚡ Welcome Wagon

⚡ Wine connoisseur

⚡ Wingman

⚡ Wizard of Oz

⚡ "Wolf" (from the Movie *Pulp Fiction*)

⚡ Yellow pages

You can expect your mission, at first, to fit like a new pair of jeans. Perhaps a little stiff ... maybe a bit too snug ... could even be scratchy. So don't be afraid to live with yours a while. Feel free to make adjustments. You have the rest of your life to tailor it.

My bias is that the *real* underlying missions don't change, but our understanding of them can evolve. So you may recognize a whole new facet of your mission as you age and your challenges change. You can play with the wording as much as you like, of course. It's the deeper, slippery and hard-to-describe meaning that sticks. A mission is like an anchor, but it's a *sea anchor*. Rather than "anchoring" you to one place, like a conventional anchor, a sea anchor does for you what it does for boats: it helps you weather the storm. Boats use a sea anchor to keep them from turning broadside to the waves and being overwhelmed by then. Your mission can keep you afloat and on course when the world tries to drag you under.

Remember: you've been living your mission all your life; you just may not have articulated it very clearly. Importantly, living your mission should give you energy and joy. If it doesn't, it's not *really* your mission.

## EnergyThink: Do... or Do Not.

"Try not. Do... or do not. There is no try," says Yoda in *Star Wars: The Empire Strikes Back*. If you've read this far and don't have a mission yet, now is the time to put down the book, pick up the pencil and write one.

Begin by converting your vocab list into a sentence and then come up with two or three words that capture the idea. Or, try it the other way around: pick a word or a phrase and explain why it works for you.

Go ahead and flip the identity switch ... see if it changes your life.

# 32

# Using Your Mission: The Big D

— — — — — — — — — — — — — — — —

**"Choose the job you love and you will never
have to work a day in your life." —Confucius**

— — — — — — — — — — — — — — — —

SO NOW YOU'VE DUG A LITTLE DEEPER INTO YOUR TOOL BOX AND
discovered this mission lying there in the bottom. It's not new; it's been
there all along. But maybe you've not been using it consciously. Let's work
on that.

Like any compass, it points in one direction. Of course, you don't
always want to go north. Few of us have the luxury of doing what our
mission calls us to do all day, every day. Life just isn't like that.

Some folks think their mission is for The "Big D" Decisions in Life. I
don't disagree, but I apply mine almost every day. Before we get to The
Everyday Uses, let's take a look at some of The Big Decisions:

⚡ You've got two job offers; which one do you choose? How do you decide?

⚡ You're trying to pick a college major; how do you select from the dozens
offered?

⚡ The guy in the job interview asks you, "Why do you want this job?"
What do you say?

⚡ Your spouse would dearly like to move to Manhattan. Good move?

⚡ You've just been promoted or hired; your new team is wondering
whether they can trust you. What should you do?

⚡ Your retirement date is looming. What will you do with your free time?

⚡ The executive recruiter on the phone is promising you a great opportunity at a new organization. Should you be excited?

⚡ Your current job pays you a lot of money, but you're bored or stressed and you never see your children. Is it time for a change? To what?

⚡ There is a "pink slip" in your inbox. You've never had to look for a job before. What should you do next?

⚡ Your best friend just won a trip around the world and invites you along; it will take two months. Should you go?

The answer to all of these questions are more questions: What does your mission tell you to do? What gives you energy? What would be more fun? Which decision makes you happier? In short, which is "you" and which is somebody else? The best recipe for real "success" is to do what you love.

## Beware the Decision Traps

Watch out for three traps:

⚡ The **money** and other assorted, related temptations like a cool city, nice office, a car, etc. One clearly established fact is that money can't buy happiness. Making money is relatively easy compared to being happy. Follow your mission: ultimately, you can probably do *both*.

⚡ The fact that you would be "**good at it**." One of worst curses is to be really good at something you don't like to do. And an *even worse* curse is to be able to make a lot of money doing it as well.

⚡ It would be **easy**. If it's not a challenge, you'll be bored soon. Do you want to spend your life bored? You didn't come so far and work so hard to be bored.

## What Would the Coach Say?

How does this work? Well, for example, let's apply one of my favorite missions, "Second Half Coach," to some of the questions above. If you were a "Second Half Coach," you might think this way:

⚡ Which job to choose? The turnaround with great potential where you can motivate a discouraged team.

⚡ Which major? The ones that seem like they would not only be fun, but would also give you the tools to be a better "coach."

⚡ The move? Sure, if there would be opportunity for you to use your mission there.

⚡ What do you tell your new team? "I know we're facing some big challenges; that's why I took this job. Together we can win."

⚡ Retiring? It's just the "Second Half" of your life. Now, you're more free than ever to live your mission.

⚡ The headhunter? You'll be asking the questions that tell you whether the job is a good fit for you. Think of the opportunity as a new player you might want to recruit.

⚡ Leave your job? Yes, if you have somewhere to go that's closer to your mission. Start looking for that. Run *toward* something; not away from something. That's what a good game plan is all about.

⚡ The layoff? It's one of the best opportunities of your life. Now, you have to think about next steps. You wouldn't have changed your game if you were ahead. You were *made* for tough situations like this one.

⚡ The trip? Fight the tendency to say that you don't have the time; you're too busy; you have other responsibilities. Pretend a spotter up in the stands saw an opening on the field you couldn't see at ground level. In the end, our biggest regrets are often not the things we did; it's the things we didn't do but could have.

## The Ikigai: An Elegant Mission Tool

How does all this fit together? Many of us like pictures that make the words clearer. I know I do. The Japanese have an elegant visual tool: the concept of Ikigai, which translates "a reason for being." An Ikigai looks like a hyper-complicated Venn diagram. Ikigai is at the intersection of what you love, what you're good at, what the world needs, and what you can be paid for. It reflects passion, mission, profession and vocation.

Imagine making four lists, one for each for passion, mission, profession and vocation. Your "Ikigai" is what is common to all four. Don't be surprised if, at first blush, the four lists seem mutually exclusive. Your niche may not be so obvious.

One of the biggest challenges is describing what you put on the list. For example, let's say you can draw and you love to do it. That clearly falls in both the "that which you are good at" circle and the "that which you love" circle, so it's definitely in the area marked "passion."

Is it also in the "profession" area? If you define "profession" as "artist," the answer may be "no." Yet there are many professions (designer, architect, illustrator) that also use that skill. What's more, you don't need to stop there. For example, David Sibbet, a renowned meeting facilitator, uses his drawing skills to great effect in helping people "see" issues more clearly. There are many other professions where drawing talent can be a great asset.

> **If it meets the passion, profession, vocation, and mission standards, it may well be your Ikigai.**

Of course, it's only a profession if you can get "paid" for it. Notice that I put "paid" in quotes. For most of us, getting paid means literally receiving cash for what we do. Yet there are many other forms of compensation: recognition, a nice warm feeling, personal satisfaction, improved relationships, giving back, etc. This circle isn't just about making a living… it's about making a life.

Does the world need it? Is it your vocation? Again, don't confuse what you *DO*, from a mission standpoint, with a job. Does the world need another artist? Maybe not. Could the world use many more "David Sibbets"—who help people understand each other and solve problems better? You bet.

So, in the end, is your drawing skill related to your mission? Is it an important part of what you *DO*? If it meets the passion, profession, vocation, and mission standards, it may well be your Ikigai.

## EnergyThink: What Do You Do, Coach?

Living your mission is the power of *who you are doing what you do*. How you apply that mission can change dramatically over the course of your life. In *Falling Upward: A Spirituality for the Two Halves of Life*, Richard Rohr argues that, in the "first half" of life, we focus on "creating an identity, seeking security and forging relationships." Essentially, it's the lower levels of Maslow's famous Hierarchy of Needs.

Maslow believed that the lowest level of need was physiological (food, water, shelter, etc.); then came safety (security, protection); then social needs (sense of belonging and love); then esteem (self-esteem, recognition, status) and finally "self actualization" (self-development and realization, or, as the Army used to say "Be All You Can Be.").

In the "second half," though, we move beyond the "lower" issues, Rohr says, often abandoning the old frameworks that supported us. In the second half, he says, we mature, broaden our perspective, grow and transform. We move higher on the Maslow pyramid in many ways. It is a courageous and often dangerous leap. The great leaders, artists, and thinkers have all made it to the "second half." Look around: so have many of the people you admire most. (And notice how the others are stuck in the lower, more materialistic, comfort-centered levels.)

So, just for practice, pretend you're the "Second Half Coach" for your life. Imagine a "team" inside of you consisting of beliefs, skills, talents, insights, assumptions, and experiences:

⚡ Before the season, whom do you want on your "team"? Which positions do you need filled? Whom should you cut? What's the game plan?

⚡ In the middle of the season—or even a game—what do you need to change? Practices? Players off and on the bench? Plays? Tactics?

⚡ After the season, need new equipment? New stadium? Time for a new team? Are you even in the right sport?

# 33

# The Value of Values

"I would not give a fig for the simplicity
this side of complexity, but I would give my
life for the simplicity on the other side of
complexity." —Oliver Wendell Holmes, Jr.

WHY DOES YOUR COMPANY HAVE A LIST OF VALUES? IS IT BECAUSE...

**a.** The CEO went to a workshop on leadership and they told him he needed values?

**b.** There was a blank space on the wall/website/annual report and the marketing guys said to fill it with "values"?

**c.** The board compliance committee needed something to do?

**d.** It's the way the company makes key decisions?

For surprisingly few companies, the answer is "d." If you spend any time browsing company websites or visiting company headquarters, you probably have seen the values "lists" prominently displayed. Sometimes, you undoubtedly have had the visceral feeling: "That's just not true." Here is a list of popular values:

⚡ **Integrity**—What does that mean?

⚡ **Honesty**—Really? Is that reflected in the last ad campaign?

⚡ **Excellence**—And how is that measured?

⚡ **Innovation**—Is that why the list of values is the same as everybody else's?

⚡ **Teamwork**—Is the customer on the team?

⚡ **Trust**—And how do they earn that?

⚡ **Respect**—How long is the average customer hold time in the call center?

⚡ **Quality**—Will they give back every penny of the money if the customer is not satisfied?

⚡ **Winning**—Clearly, *they* are winning…is the customer?

Here's the ultimate test: ask anybody in the company to name the values without peeking at the list.

## We're Creatures of Our Values

Don't get me wrong. I am sure most companies really *do* live their values. They are just *not* the values on the wall or the website. Most individuals are the same way. We are all creatures of our values. Our decisions and actions reflect our values. When we decide or act, a little scale in our heads chooses the best route for us, according to our values. It can be a complex process, but it happens quickly.

> **I am sure most companies really do live their values. They are just not the values on the wall or the website.**

We have hundreds, if not thousands, of values. Often, though, we've so internalized our values that we're not even conscious of them. I have many times asked ethics classes to name their values. I usually get about five (integrity, accountability, honesty, compassion and hard work top the list). Personally, my values list also includes fast bicycles, fishing, sunny days, single malt scotch and Reese's Peanut Butter Cups.

Socrates said that ethics is essentially a set of standards, based on core values, that dictate how we should act or decide. He contended that ethics was the most interesting subject people could discuss. (Of course, that was before Monday Night Football.) Why is ethics so interesting? Different people have different values. It's why, for example, there are two sets of fans at every football game. Ask a die hard fan what he or she thinks of the "other" team and you'll often get a lot of emotional energy…and not all of it "good."

Here is a set of common "values"... that I label common ethical "viruses":

⚡ Most people cannot be trusted

⚡ I'm not worth much

⚡ I'm better than most people

⚡ Might makes right

⚡ If it feels good, do it

⚡ Winning is everything

⚡ My needs are more important than anybody else's

⚡ Most people care more about themselves than anyone else

⚡ People of other (races, religions, nationalities) are not as good as people of my (race, religion, nationality).

Do you see many examples of these in the world around you? You bet. They're probably a lot more common than the typical "on the wall" values.

This is not an infallible approach, but I tend to *believe* the values that sound like they were built for the company or the individual. For example, here are the values of the successful online retailer Zappos:

⚡ Deliver WOW Through Service

⚡ Embrace and Drive Change

⚡ Create Fun and A Little Weirdness

⚡ Be Adventurous, Creative, and Open-Minded

⚡ Pursue Growth and Learning

⚡ Build Open and Honest Relationships With Communication

⚡ Build a Positive Team and Family Spirit

⚡ Do More With Less

⚡ Be Passionate and Determined

⚡ Be Humble.

Here are Google's:

- ⚡ Focus on the user and all else will follow
- ⚡ It's best to do one thing really, really well
- ⚡ Fast is better than slow
- ⚡ Democracy on the web works
- ⚡ You don't need to be at your desk to need an answer
- ⚡ You can make money without doing evil
- ⚡ There's always more information out there
- ⚡ The need for information crosses all borders
- ⚡ You can be serious without a suit
- ⚡ Great just isn't good enough.

How credible are these lists? If you've ever done business with these companies, have you experienced those values? That doesn't mean that the companies live them perfectly; nobody is perfect. But you can identify those values much more easily than "excellence," "integrity," or "teamwork."

Here is my list of core values:

- ⚡ **Spirit.** From the Holy Spirit to school spirit, I like "spirit." I value the "old college try." I admire people who pick themselves up and try again, like Teddy Roosevelt's dust-covered fighter in the arena and Vince Lombardi's fallen football player.

- ⚡ **Light.** As an educator, I love it when I see the light bulbs go on in the heads in the class or the audience. As a reporter, I worked to shine a light on complex and often hidden information valuable to my readers.

- ⚡ **Energy.** Well, you know how I feel about that. You're reading this book.

- ⚡ **Endurance.** I believe in plugging along, well beyond what everybody (including me) thought was likely or even possible. I value tenacity. Persistence and perseverance pay. (I admire indefatigability, too, but I can't pronounce it dependably.)

⚡ **Productivity.** *My mission is to use the magic of communication to help people live happier, more rewarding and more productive lives.* It's important to be both productive and efficient. It's what good marketing is all about. That's why my company is called Good Ground Consulting: "The seed that fell on good ground multiplied a hundredfold." (Luke 8:8)

> It's important to be both productive and efficient. It's what good marketing is all about.

You'll notice that the list spells the acronym SLEEP. Not only does that make it easier for me to remember, I value sleep, too. I try to live my values every day in every way: on the bike, on the computer, in front of an audience or a room of students, with my colleagues and clients.

## EnergyThink: What Are Your REAL Values?

"We are the clumsy stewards of our own souls," writes Richard Rohr in *Falling Upward: A Spirituality for the Two Halves of Life*. Wresting energy and direction from values buried deep inside can be messy and challenging, but worth the effort.

⚡ What are your *real* values? Look again at the list you created above in the mission exercise. Which values really drive your life?

⚡ Do you like the list? Perhaps you're proud of some values… and others, well, not so much.

⚡ Can you change those values? How would you do that? A word of caution: it could change your life.

# 34

# Using Your Mission and Values —All the Time

---

**"I cannot teach anyone anything; I can only make him think." —Socrates**

---

YOU DON'T HAVE TO KEEP YOUR MISSION OR CORE VALUES ON ICE, waiting for The Big Decisions. If you look, you'll see lots of chances to use them.

- ⚡ Would it be better to go to a movie or read a book? (Which movie? Which book?)

- ⚡ Do you want to work late or go to the gym?

- ⚡ Which charitable donations should you make?

- ⚡ For which organizations should you volunteer?

- ⚡ Do you have time/energy for that meeting?

- ⚡ Should you have the conversation at the water cooler?

- ⚡ Are you comfortable with your schedule?

- ⚡ How are you spending the weekend?

- ⚡ Where should you go on vacation?

You have to make these and countless other value- and mission-related decisions every day. What's more, your VIPs (remember them, the people you *want* to help?), energy buddies and vampires are also going to have something to say about how you live your mission. Will you say "yes" or "no"?

Perhaps this is a good place to back away a bit and look at your life in terms of your *real* core values. Have you been living them? If you think about it a bit, you'll probably discover that the answer is "yes"—if you're honest with yourself about what they really are.

Here's a tool I use to look at my values... and my life. As you can see in Illustration #5, I've made a matrix with my key values, "SLEEP," along the left side and the decades of my life along the top. For each key value, I've given myself an example of how I've succeed (there isn't room for all the failures). I've also included a "theme" that describes what was going on at a very high level during that decade. The matrix is far from complete, but it helps me realize what an important role my values have played in my life. Ironically, most of the time I wasn't even thinking about values. I was just living... and following my energy.

> **Look at your life in terms of your real core values. Have you been living them?**

If you decide to build such a matrix, you don't have to use decades along the top side of your matrix. Years work just fine. Also, you don't have to pick even amounts of time. You could pick tenure in a job, years at school or in a particular city, etc.

## EnergyThink: Where Does Your Energy Flow?

⚡ Step back and look at your life as a series of energy flows, swirling around your mission, driven by your real values. You don't make The Big Decisions every day... or do you?

⚡ Have you noticed that your life is driven by the constant flow of micro-decisions you are constantly (and often unconsciously) making?

⚡ Do you have to obsess about this? Not unless you want to. Most of us have a little Geiger Counter inside that buzzes when things either give or take away energy. If you're feeling the "bad buzz," perhaps it's worth trying to figure out why.

⚡ If you're feeling the "good buzz," what can you do to enhance and extend it?

| | 1950s | 1960s | 1970s |
|---|---|---|---|
| **Theme** | Becoming a child; learning to be a person | From child to man; learning to be an adult | Successful journalist; learning to tell a story |
| **Spirit** | Family values; Play alone; Italian heritage | Get into good college; cub reporter; succeed in extra curricular activities/sports; fall in love | More serious relationships; deeper faith experience; journalistic values; father dies |
| **Light** | Serious reader | "A" student; trophy athlete; original orator; campus protests; shift to liberal politics | Princeton and Harvard; Washington and Detroit; story telling impact |
| **Energy** | Lots; maybe even too much | Vast increase in every type via demanding activities | Increasing intellectual demands; bike racing |
| **Endurance** | Enjoy tackling long-term "projects" | Relentless pursuit of success in every area | Totally driven life; constant motion machine |
| **Productivity** | Help my father in his business and do-it-yourself projects | Success in and out of school | Two academic degrees; productive Wall Street Journal reporter |

*Illustration #5: We all live according to our "values"—the things that we value. But those "values" aren't often the typical ones we see on websites, office walls, the Boy Scout Oath, and the Golden Rule. Most of us have hundreds of values—and a handful that really drive our lives. Think about drawing a matrix like this one that gives examples of how you lived your most important values over your life—"era by era." In my case, I've divided my life by decades according to themes, but you can define your "eras" any way you like.*

|  | 1980s | 1990s | 2000s | 2010s |
|---|---|---|---|---|
| **Theme** | Father, non-profit executive; learning about family and faith | Successful businessman; Learning to lead teams | On my own; learning to run my own race | Life veteran; learning to discover and teach |
| **Spirit** | Quit Journal for Catholic Charities; marriage; children; enormous financial anxiety | Difficult transition to "business values" | Take major life/ work steps; own business; divorce | Do more of what matters; more joy in work |
| **Light** | Insights into spouse relationship; child rearing; leadership; advocacy; innovation; the church | Gradually learn three businesses; master transition to business | Freedom; costs and benefits | Focus on helping others "see the light" |
| **Energy** | Very stretched and stressed; working hard to be good dad, cheerlead at work | Vast amounts of time/energy sucked into business | Big energy boost when stressors change; biking more seriously | More energy for adventure while I still can |
| **Endurance** | Bike, fishing, hunting, child activities are balances to work/ life stresses | Keep plugging to pay for schools, house, life style | Commitment to business means working hard to stay afloat | Endurance over speed - 90% mental 10% fuel economy |
| **Productivity** | Highly productive at work: many new programs for poor; struggle to pay the bills | Make a lot more money; reduce financial stress somewhat | Kids through college; firm increasingly successful; randonneuring | Successful teacher/ trainer of my own stuff; good pro bono projects |

# 35

# Spiritual Energy and Crisis

---

**"With training, equipment, and the WILL TO SURVIVE, you will find you can overcome any obstacle you may face. You will survive. You must understand the emotional states associated with survival; 'knowing thyself' is extremely important in a survival situation. It bears directly on how well you cope with serious stresses, anxiety, pain, injury, illness, cold, heat, thirst, hunger, fatigue, sleep deprivation, boredom, loneliness and isolation." —U.S. Army Survival Handbook**

---

"SERIOUS STRESSES, ANXIETY, PAIN, INJURY, ILLNESS, COLD, HEAT, thirst, hunger, fatigue, sleep deprivation, boredom, loneliness and isolation." Does that sound a little like your life? I've always found it interesting that the Army Rangers, who jump out of airplanes into hostile territory, choose this murderous list—and not the enemy—as the biggest threat. Since their lives depend upon it, the Rangers know well that often the enemy is the least of their worries.

Their prescription for success includes the spiritual-sounding "knowing thyself." How you behave in a crisis can define who you really are.

Charles Duhigg, a *New York Times* reporter who wrote *The Power of Habit*, notes that "a good crisis is a terrible thing to waste." Often, it takes a crisis to jar us out of our bad habits, personal or corporate. But first, of course, we have to survive the crisis.

In any crisis, look to your mission. It is your compass and your anchor. To borrow a phrase from iconoclastic author Nassim Nicholas Taleb, your mission is "antifragile."[1] Plans are fragile, mostly because we can't see the future and many things can derail a plan. In a crisis, though, you can always go to your mission. Often, there won't be any choice. "In a crisis, don't hide behind anything or anybody. They're going to find you anyway," said Paul "Bear" Bryant, the legendary University of Alabama football coach.

## Surviving into "Thin Air"

One person who was "found," but left for dead three times is Beck Weathers. The Texas pathologist was part of the ill-fated 1996 Everest expedition chronicled in Jon Krakeuer's best-seller *Into Thin Air: A Personal Account of the Mt. Everest Disaster.*

A few years after the disaster, I had dinner with Weathers prior to a speech I invited him to give at a sales meeting. Weathers is both inspiring and sobering. I have carried his image with me on every mountain I've climbed. I recall his story with every tough challenge I face.

He lost an arm, the fingers on his other hand and most of his face after being stranded in the Death Zone on the mountain with a wind-chill of more than 100 degrees below zero. Far from his base camp, he had gone deep into hypothermia, a condition no one is supposed to survive. "It is a one-way ticket to death," he said.

> **I would keep moving until I walked into that camp, I fell down and could not stand, or I walked off the face of that mountain.**

But, he said that a "miracle" occurred for him on the mountain: "Simply stated, I opened my eyes…directly in front of my face is my gloveless dead hand…it has the marvelous effect of focusing my attention.

"I could see my family before me and I knew that if I did not stand, I would spend an eternity upon that spot…. I struggled to my feet … and I decided …if I fell down, I would get up. And if I fell down again, I would get up. And I would keep moving until I walked into that camp, I fell down and could not stand, or I walked off the face of that mountain.

"And as I began that journey, both of my hands were completely frozen. My face had been destroyed by the cold. I was profoundly hypothermic. I had not eaten in three days. I had no water. I was lost and almost completely blind. A lesser person could be discouraged. But you can't sweat that small stuff. You have to *focus*."

As he staggered through the snow, he said he was surprised he was not afraid. Instead, there was a deeper, spiritual motivation: "There was an overwhelming sense of melancholy that I would not say good bye. That I would never again say 'I love you' to my wife. That I would never again hold my children. It was just not acceptable."

His climbing partners were told to leave him behind because he would die anyway. But he didn't die, making an incredible descent that included the highest helicopter rescue in history.

His message: "I'm an entirely ordinary individual... If I can survive that which is unsurvivable, so can you. There exists within each of us an enormous well of strength—if we will but believe it, reach out, grasp it, and use it....You've got to have an anchor. It can be your friends, your colleagues, your God or it can be, as it was for me, my family."

## Above the Clouds

In the world of climbing, Anatoli Boukreev was a legend. The Russian high-attitude mountaineer saved some lives during the fateful Everest climb—and was criticized for not saving more, including Weathers. He was killed the following year in an avalanche on Annapurna.

In *Above the Clouds*, a collection of his writings, he talks about descending mountains while watching other climbers continue on up... to certain death. He writes:

I wondered at the power that the mountains exert over us, calling people to push themselves to undergo such tests of courage, strength and purity....I realized that I needed these trials and struggles, that they are important to me. It is with myself I struggle in this life, not with the mountains....and the road that we choose to follow in life depends less on the surrounding world than on our spirit—the internal voice that pushes one to seek new challenges.[2]

## Judgment... on Kilimanjaro

When I neared the top of my Kilimanjaro climb, I could feel the effort and lack of oxygen clouding my judgment. At one point, I thought I was feeling pretty good—and challenged one of the guides to a footrace. He laughed and we took off up the mountain. I made it about 20 paces. I felt as though someone had stuffed a pillow down my throat.

The guide just chuckled as I gasped in vain for air. After that, I began to feel the eerie, but common climber's sensation of walking under water.

I could see the peak ahead and I was conscious of it coming closer as I trudged along between the mountain's towering glaciers. Everything seemed fuzzy and in slow motion, like in those corny romantic scenes in 1960's movies. Unlike the climbers in the 1996 Everest disaster, I wasn't marching towards my doom (after all, I was *two miles* lower than Everest's peak). Yet I could still feel the stubborn single-mindedness of "Summit Fever."

> **You don't have to be a serious climber to hear the Siren song of the voice in your head: "Higher... higher... higher."**

Funny thing: at the top, I didn't feel much of the elation that I thought I would. Maybe I was too tired and oxygen-depleted. Maybe I was too worried about getting down. Maybe *Dilbert* author Scott Adams was right about how ultimately unsatisfying goals can be.

## EnergyThink: What Is Your "Internal Voice" Pushing You to Do?

You don't have to be a serious climber to hear the Siren song of the voice in your head: "Higher... higher... higher." I've climbed a few mountains in my life, but the steepest pitches have always been inside me... and not on the hillside. Sometimes we seek the challenge, but often it is thrust upon us in the form of a crisis.

⚡ Are you confronting a crisis now? How does it compare with past challenges?

⚡ Do you anticipate one in the future? Will you look for one?

⚡ What resources, which "energy tanks" will you draw upon?

⚡ How will you access the most powerful energy source: the spiritual?

# 36

## Discovering Your Personal Mascot

---

**"A very great vision is needed, and the man
who has it must follow it as the eagle seeks the
deepest blue of the sky." —Crazy Horse[1]**

---

YOU HAVE A MISSION; IT'S AN IMPORTANT PART OF YOUR IDENTITY.
Now, you need a new name or "mascot" to add more dimension and energy.

I mentioned earlier how the great chief Crazy Horse believed that his
name had such power he could not be injured in battle. The notion that a
name brings power is an old one.

Tribes, for example, have names and we are all tribal. For example, I
live in Baltimore where there is the Orioles Tribe for baseball fans and
the Ravens Tribe for football fans. The mascots of those organizations
unquestionably generate energy for the teams—and the spectators who
follow them. There is a brisk business in Orioles and Ravens paraphernalia
for exactly this reason.

Now, think about your name. How did your parents select your first
name? What is the power of the reputation that your last name carries?
Would you change your name? Why or why not?

Most people do not select their own names. I'm not suggesting that you
legally change yours, although many people have done so to good effect.
I am recommending, though, that you go through a miniature version of
the powerful process that the Native Americans used to pick their own
names—and to use the process to boost your energy.

For many tribes, the selection of a name was a rite of passage for a
young person. Often, it meant heading off to a desolate place and going
without sleep, food or water for days. At some point, the person would
have a vision (or a hallucination, depending on your bias). From that

vision, the person would draw a name: Crazy Horse, Red Cloud, Sitting Bull, etc.

## Naming *UP*: This Won't Hurt... Much

Don't worry: I won't ask you to suffer that much. Instead, just imagine you're going on a very pleasant walk. It can be in the woods, along the beach, in the mountains, or even through make-believe land—or on the moon. Wherever you're comfortable going for a quiet, imaginative stroll is just fine. Just be relaxed and open.

On your "walk," you're going to see something. Often, I find that some kind of an animal works best, but it can be anything that stops you and arrests your attention. If you see an animal (real or fictional, like a phoenix or mermaid), perhaps you look into its eyes and identify with it in some way. Perhaps it makes some kind of familiar gesture. The idea is to adopt an image with which you're comfortable. That animal or thing is "half" your mascot name. It's the "noun" (for example, horse, cloud, bull).

> **Now that you have a new mascot name, what will you do with it?**

Next, you need an adjective (for example, crazy, red, sitting). You can make up one yourself, of course. Often, though, it's useful to share the noun with others, explain why you chose it, and have a discussion with them about what a fitting adjective might be. I find the discussion leads to better choices.

Now that you have a new mascot name, what will you do with it? Should you wear it on a name tag around your neck? Tattoo it on your arm? Only if you're into that sort of thing. Mostly, it's your own special name. It's a little like T.S. Eliot wrote in *Old Possum's Book of Practical Cats*:

> But above and beyond there's still one name left over,
> And that is the name that you never will guess;
> *The name that no human research can discover—*
> But THE CAT HIMSELF KNOWS, and will never confess.

Your new name should do for you exactly the same thing that powerful names do for sports teams, military units, cars, and neighborhoods. It's part of your brand. It should give you more energy, especially in that hard to define "spiritual" category.

## The Dragon and the Bright Hawk

For example, once, when I took a friend through the mascot process, she chose "beaver" as her animal. Like the beaver, she is hard-working, industrious, always busy and liked the water. But the image was kind of wet and muddy and cold and didn't really resonate with her sunny personality.

"What do you see, Beaver, when you look around?" I asked.

"Water. Trees. Mud. Sticks," she replied.

"How about when you look up?"

"Bridges in the sky," was her arresting response.

"Whoa," I observed. "That's not very 'beaverish.' Beavers don't fly."

She decided to think about the idea for a while. When I saw her next, she had a much more powerful image: "I'm a Dragon."

My mascot name is "Bright Hawk." I love the way hawks fly, swooping down on their prey. It reminds me of zooming downhill on my bicycle—fast, free and effortless. I also appreciate the fact that they are known for their vision and their ability to see clearly from high above. I hope to be able to grasp both the big picture and the important details of any issue.

I chose the adjective "bright" because it means both smart and colorful (characteristics I admire in both their literal and figurative senses). I like the crisp, monosyllabic sound.

Notice that the name does not have to make logical or literal sense. For example, if you pick "horse" you don't also have to pick "galloping" or if you choose "salmon" you don't have to select "swimming." Hawks are not necessarily "bright." The important thing is that the name works for you.

> **Notice that the name does not have to make logical or literal sense.**

I find that my mascot name is a good "totem" of traits I admire. Like a flag for a troop of soldiers, it's a symbol of who I am. A bonus for me is that I often see hawks when I am driving or riding.

"Hello, little brother," I say, greeting them as the Native Americans might and enjoying a little throb of energy every time.

When I am working with groups, I'll often combine the process of finding a mission and finding a mascot name. I find the processes often go together in very interesting ways. Frequently, the values people articulate in the mission process are reflected in some innovative way in the naming process.

And, speaking of innovation, there's my *favorite* mascot name, from a class I taught in Colorado: "Runs with Scissors."

## EnergyThink: What's Your Mascot Name?

⚡ Somebody just paid you a huge compliment. In response, you say, "Well, just call me…" What should they call you?

⚡ Like many people, you've probably experienced the power of mascots. Almost no sports team, at any level, goes without one. What's yours?

# PART SEVEN

# Moving Toward a More Balanced, Happier Life

# 37

# Energy, Mission, Balance, and Happiness

---

**"We hold these truths to be self-evident, that all men are created equal, that they are endowed by their Creator with certain unalienable Rights, that among these are Life, Liberty and the pursuit of Happiness." —The Declaration of Independence**

---

THE SECRET OF A POWERFUL, BALANCED, HAPPY LIFE IS USING YOUR energy to live your mission. According to the Declaration of Independence, we have the right to "pursue happiness." It's a little bit like a fishing license. A fishing license gives you the right to go fishing, but it doesn't give you fish.

History tells us that the Virginian George Mason wanted the Declaration to read the "right to life, liberty and property," but Ben Franklin thought we should reach a bit higher than that, God bless him.

So, this raises the great question, "What makes you happy?" Philosophers and scholars have been pondering that for many years, with many potential answers. One thing that they all agree upon (and the research data supports) is that money can't buy it. Indeed, after some point, additional money adds little additional enjoyment. George Bernard Shaw said it perfectly: "You can easily find people who are ten times as rich at 60 as they were at 20; but not one of them will tell you that they are ten times as happy."

Positive psychology guru Martin Seligman devoted his life to the question. In his book *Flourishing*, he attempts an answer. It's PERMA:

⚡ **Positive emotion/pleasure:** Did it feel good? Are you satisfied with your life?

⚡ **Engagement/flow:** Did time stop for you? Were you completely absorbed by the task?

⚡ **Relationships:** How do you relate to other people?

⚡ **Meaning:** Do you belong to/serve something that you believe is bigger than yourself?

⚡ **Accomplishment:** Do you pursue success, accomplishment, winning, achievement or mastery for its own sake?[1]

Notice how well the concept of *mission* fits with Seligman's PERMA/Happiness concept.

⚡ **Positive emotion/pleasure:** You LOVE your mission.

⚡ **Engagement/flow:** You're *so* into this that you lose track of time.

⚡ **Relationships:** You'll be drawn to and attract people who need what your mission offers.

⚡ **Meaning:** Mission gives purpose to your life.

⚡ **Accomplishment:** You're most likely to succeed in areas related to your mission.

If you want to be happy, balanced and successful, just live your mission.

## EnergyThink: Your Own PERMA

Match your life with Seligman's PERMA concept.

⚡ **Positive emotion/pleasure:** You LOVE doing this: _____

⚡ **Engagement/flow:** You're *so* into this, _____, that you lose track of time.

⚡ **Relationships:** You'll be drawn to and attract people who need you when you're doing this: _____.

⚡ **Meaning:** This _____ gives purpose to your life.

⚡ **Accomplishment:** You're most likely to succeed doing this: _____

# 38

## Energy and Leadership... and Goliath

— — — — — — — — — — — — — — — — —

**"Then Saul clothed David in his own tunic, putting a bronze helmet on his head and arming him with a coat of mail. David also girded himself with Saul's sword over the tunic. He walked with difficulty, however, since he had never tried armor before. He said to Saul, "I cannot go in these, because I have never tried them before." So he took them off. Then, staff in hand, David selected five smooth stones from the wadi and put them in the pocket of his shepherd's bag. With his sling also ready to hand, he approached the Philistine." —1 Samuel 17:38-40**

— — — — — — — — — — — — — — — — —

IN HIS BEST-SELLER *DAVID AND GOLIATH*, MALCOLM GLADWELL theorizes that no one observing the classic biblical battle would have been surprised to see David vanquish his giant foe. "Artillery beats infantry," Gladwell says simply.

Well, maybe. But the story has resonated for centuries primarily because of the possible misconception that David was over-matched. To me, it's David's energy, not just his sure-shooting sling, that wins the day. That energy infected and inspired a nation for four decades during his reign and, arguably, for centuries more. He became one of history's most famous leaders not only because of his one-day heroism, but because of a lifetime of good energy.

David's historic encounter is a classic turnaround. It's one of the most famous examples of what can happen when all four types of energy—PIES—come to bear against giant problems:

⚡ The *physical* energy of a hardy little shepherd;

⚡ The *intellectual* energy of a sound strategy, proven in his boyhood battles against flock-threatening beasts;

⚡ The *emotional* energy of a young patriot amidst the terrified vampires of his own army, including its king;

⚡ The *spiritual* energy of boy who believes that his God is on his side.

What was true for David in his time is also true for us in ours, especially if we are leaders. If you are a leader, you have an extra energy obligation. You get to share yours. And, because you're the leader, your energy is *especially contagious*:

⚡ If you are sharing *positive energy in abundance*, you are on your way to killing any number of problematic giants.

⚡ If it's a lot of *negative energy*, you are the problem.

⚡ If it's *low energy and positive*, well, it's just like trying to do anything with a weak battery: might work, might not, and it will take a lot longer.

⚡ If it's *low energy and negative*, you are slowly draining everybody else's batteries.

Again, energy feeds on itself. If you care about the *time* it takes to get done what you want done, check your battery and your team's. Are you balanced? Are you charging on all four types of energy?

## EnergyThink: What Kind of a Leader Are You?

There are many different kinds of leaders who use, diffuse, and abuse many kinds of energy. An interesting model for leadership comes from Robert Quinn's great book, *Deep Change*. He posits four leadership styles along two axes: internal versus external focus; flexibility versus stability:

⚡ Vision setter: high flexibility with an external focus;

⚡ Taskmaster: high stability with an external focus;

⚡ Analyzer: high stability with an internal focus;

⚡ Motivator: high flexibility with an internal focus.

In a sense, he's describing what fuels the energy pump for each type of leader. Innovation feeds energy to the Vision Setter, high performance juices the Taskmaster, the Analyzer loves efficiency, and the Motivator wants everyone happy and growing.

Few leaders exist purely in one quadrant.

As an energy leader, it's time to gather your "five smooth stones." Just as David armed himself for battle, you have to decide how you will appear before your Goliath—and the "army" of folks relying on you. At this point, humility helps a lot. Note that David just needed one stone, but picking up only one would have been a little presumptuous. He was prepared to make the first one count…and to reload if he missed.

> **As an energy leader, it's time to gather your "five smooth stones."**

⚡ How do you feel about your leadership energy "style"?

⚡ How well does your "style" match what your job is today?

⚡ How well does your "style" fit in your current organization?

⚡ What could you do to make your life as a leader better match your "style"?

⚡ What could you change to make your leadership style better able to defeat the giants you're facing?[1]

# 39

# Listening for "The Call"

---

**"Go and find it. Go and look behind the Ranges—
Something lost behind the Ranges. Lost and waiting
for you. Go!" —Rudyard Kipling, *The Explorer***

---

THE CAREER SEARCH PIONEER RICHARD NELSON BOLLES, AUTHOR OF
*What Color is Your Parachute?*, sold millions of copies to baby boomers
frantically scrambling to find their way. It's still a popular book, joined by
hundreds of other similar self-help volumes.

Reading a book can make the light go on in your head. So can a lot of
other experiences. Around the next corner can be the "ah-ha!" moments,
the epiphanies and the surprises that trigger the life-changing insights.

I had one of those in March 1979. While at work, my father died of
a sudden, severe heart attack. It was his first and last. I remember my
mother's tearful voice on the phone: "Daddy's dead…" she began. For me,
as a young reporter, it was one of the most important headlines of my life.

At the time, I was working for *The Wall Street Journal* covering economics in Washington. From a career standpoint, it was a terrific job.
Although I felt a little restless and lived under crushing deadline pressure,
it was hard to find fault with such an influential position at such a great
publication—at the tender age of 30.

Writing economics during the Jimmy Carter Administration may have
been one of the best jobs in the profession. The country was wracked with
"stagflation," the Great Dilemma of both high inflation and low economic
growth. The *Journal's* Washington bureau was at the epicenter of the crisis
and my daily diet of depressing news might have been one of the most
closely followed stories in America.

Yet the shock of my father's death "raised my antenna," demonstrating how unbalanced my life was. It tuned my head to a different channel than the ceaseless sound of cascading economic indicators. I can't say that I was "hearing voices," but the messages of career change began to echo through my skull. I began to notice things that I hadn't noticed before. People would make chance comments that triggered torrents of introspective thoughts.

Celebrated travel writer Pico Iyer, author of *The Art of Stillness: Adventures in Going Nowhere*, uses the metaphor of viewing our lives on a huge screen—two inches from our noses. He contends we need to back up to see the entire picture, to make sense of the "slide show" of our lives, to appreciate and understand the vast wealth of experiences in our past...to restore balance. And to think about the rest of our lives.[1]

So I backed up...a lot.

I went on a week-long Jesuit retreat, just looking for a quiet time away from the constant chatter of Washington. In the silence there, I found myself bathed in a conviction that I had to leave to somehow make the world a better place. The importance of the silence can't be over estimated. You have to be really quiet to listen. As Kahil Gibran wrote in *The Prophet*:

> You talk when you cease to be at peace with your thoughts;
> and when you can no longer dwell in the solitude of your heart, you live in your lips, and sound is a diversion and a pastime.
> And in much of your talking, thinking is half-murdered. For thought is a bird of space, that in a cage of words may indeed unfold its wings but cannot fly.

## From The U.S. Treasury to a Soup Kitchen

When I returned to Washington, I submitted my resignation with no opportunities in the offing. The *Journal's* bureau chief wisely pointed out that it might be a bit rash to quit a job for which thousands of young journalists would gladly exchange their right arms.

Undeterred, I left. Three months later, I found myself working for Catholic Charities of Baltimore designing programs to address the growing problem of homelessness. A year later, we opened Our Daily Bread, a soup kitchen that became Maryland's largest and most famous. It's still going today, more than three decades later and more than 20 years after I left the agency. It has served more than seven million free meals to the hungry. When he visited Baltimore, the Pope ate there.

The privilege of working on that project is one of the cherished experiences of my life. Nothing in my seven years on the Journal staff even compares remotely to it. Had I stayed at the Journal, I would have literally never known what I missed.

Thirty-five years later, in 2015, I rode across the country to raise money for it.

What was behind my move from *The Wall Street Journal* to Catholic Charities? I don't think that I had any special "divine guidance" that isn't widely available to everybody. Indeed, that "guidance" is out there for everybody, whether one believes it comes from God, from a spark of inspiration, from pure chance or from a hiccup in one's DNA.

> **Right now, we're all missing opportunities that are just beyond our reach or vision.**

Right now, we're all missing opportunities that are just beyond our reach or vision. Like Kipling's explorer, we are settled where we are. We can't see over the mountains. It seems dangerous out there... and it probably is.

Still, there's this "itch." Perhaps it's for something specific like writing a great novel or living in an exotic place. Perhaps it's just boredom or unease. Perhaps it's watching your life slip away without any meaning.

### Listen! Listen! LISTEN!

So, here's the whole trick: you have to listen. To the little voice inside... to your conscience... to a friend... to your spouse or child. (My kids' horror or support for my career moves have been a great guiding force.) Often, the "call" seems accidental or serendipitous. It's just opportunity masquerading as pure chance. You don't have to go to a monastery to listen (although a change of scenery might help some). Solitary, quiet activities that emphasize stillness are very helpful. Just sitting in the woods, marveling at Mother Nature, works.

Look out. Look up. Find a new balance. That's it.

How do you know if what you're hearing is "right"? It's the energy that the idea generates. Not *just* an initial flash of excitement, although that's often the case. We're talking energy with legs. Energy that lasts. More energy than you experience in your current industry, career or job. Enough energy to give up the comfortable cubicle, the steady pay check, the "sure thing." Enough energy to make you move out of the rut you're in, whether it's a pleasant retirement or a desk in the C-suite, complete with golden handcuffs.

> **Look out. Look up. Find a new balance. That's it.**

In *Uncommon Genius: How Great Ideas Are Born*, Denise Shekerjian writes,

> Listen for the special music, the song that nobody else can sing but you. Your own karma badly lived is better than someone else's karma lived well. A creative person is one who enjoys, above all else, the company of his own mind.

## EnergyThink: Are You Listening?

In his daily blog, Vermont nature artist Roderick MacIver quotes Sarah Ban Breathnach in *Simple Abundance: A Daybook of Comfort and Joy*:

> Perhaps the heart of our melancholy is that we miss the person we were meant to be. We miss our authentic selves. But the good news is that even if you have ignored its overtures for decades, your authentic self has not abandoned you. Instead it has been waiting patiently for you to recognize it and reconnect. Turn away from the world this year and begin to listen.

⚡ Do you feel a tug at your anchor rope?

⚡ Does the prospect of "another day" give you energy—or drain it?

⚡ We should all be so lucky as to do everyday everything that we love to do. But are you doing anything that you enjoy and that gives you juice? What is it?

⚡ What are the things that suck your lifeblood? Can you stop?

# 40

# GO! NOW! GO!

---

**"Everybody wants to go to heaven; nobody wants to die." —Boxer Joe Louis**

---

IT IS *SO* VERY HARD TO GO.

It means abandoning the comfort zone, no matter how unbalanced it is. And, even if it's hell where you are now, it's your hell. For sure, it will be painful to go, like an operation you need, but have been putting off. There will be that agonizing moment of crisis when, standing at the edge of the high diving board, you bounce once or twice and go head first into the pool. Like...

⚡ When you put your house on the market and leave town.

⚡ When you tell your boss you're quitting.

⚡ When you ask for the divorce.

⚡ When you stop smoking and drinking.

⚡ When you join the Marines.

⚡ When you commit to run the marathon.

⚡ When you make the deposit on the trip around the world.

⚡ When you leave the firm to write the novel.

⚡ When you ask her to marry you.

⚡ When you go into the streets to protest.

⚡ When you tell your kids you're gay.

Well, what are you waiting for? Not ready yet? Not prepared? You're never prepared to do something for the first time. Let's go back to our boy David. He's a shepherd and a young one at that. He's doing menial, dirty, dry, dangerous work. Boring and often frustrating work. No military academy courses on weaponry or giant killing tactics. No merit badge for slinging. No particular preparation to pick off Goliath, much less become King of the Jews.

But the giant is here. Now.

In his famous "But, If Not" sermon in November 1967, five months before his death, Martin Luther King called on all of us to face down our giants:

> And I say to you this morning, that if you have never found something so dear and so precious to you that you will die for it, then you aren't fit to live. You may be 38 years old as I happen to be, and one day some great opportunity stands before you and calls upon you to stand up for some great principle, some great issue, some great cause--and you refuse to do it because you are afraid; you refuse to do it because you want to live longer; you're afraid that you will lose your job, or you're afraid that you will be criticized or that you will lose your popularity or you're afraid that somebody will stab you or shoot at you or bomb your house, and so you refuse to take the stand. Well you may go on and live until you are 90, but you're just as dead at 38 as you would be at 90! And the cessation of breathing in your life is but the belated announcement of an earlier death of the spirit.

> **Well you may go on and live until you are 90, but you're just as dead at 38 as you would be at 90!**

## It Will Take Time...

Yes, it will take time to make those changes, but if you've gotten this far you know that what really matters is *energy*. A lot of energy. By now, though, you know how to get more energy. It's *right there*, waiting for you to tap it. Plus, if you're doing the "right" thing—the "thing" that's aligned with your mission—you'll get the energy you need. And energy builds on itself. Life may not turn out to be nearly as tough as you fear.

Think of it: you'll be taking on your own giant and you'll be doing it your way. Like David. The way Mother Nature always intended you to do it. Remember, she has built you to *love* your mission. Like the Labrador Retriever who can't get enough fetching.

*Can you feel Mother Nature nudging you?* She's trying to push you out of the nest, whispering in your ear, "Fly! FLY!" Think of all the potential she gave you, all that unused talent, just screaming to be used. And under that talent, there's a thermonuclear generator of energy, idling away.

*But what if you fail?* That's part of life, too. You get to learn from it and get better…it's evolution. It's Mother Nature's way.

*But it's dangerous. You could get hurt.* What? Do you want to live forever? Crazy Horse rode into battle crying, "Hokahey!"—"Today is a good day to die." It wasn't a negative energy message, it was an enormously positive one. Like Martin Luther King, he was fearlessly open to all the possibilities.

*Do it for yourself.* The race is its own reward; you don't need to win to enjoy the ride. It's the system, not the goal. Do what you love. You were made for it.

## EnergyThink: Will You Roll Down the Road …or Sit on the Couch?

Okay, Energy Buddy. No more questions except the ones already in your head.

You can do it. *You're UP for it!* Good luck. Godspeed.

Hokahey!

— — — — — — — — — — — — — —

**"Do the thing and you will have the power." —Ralph Waldo Emerson**

— — — — — — — — — — — — — —

# Appendices

# Appendix I

## Greg's *Getting UP!* Checklist

— — — — — — — — — — — — — —

NOW THAT YOU'VE READ THE BOOK (OR AT LEAST SKIMMED TO THE back), here's a quick 20-question list to review before you tackle anything that will demand a lot of energy.

1. __ Is there a compelling reason to do this?
2. __ Does it align with your personal mission?
3. __ Will it make you happier in the long run?
4. __ Are you proud of this? Would you tell your mother?
5. __ Have you weighed the risks to all involved?
6. __ Have you the humility to address your weaknesses?
7. __ Can you deal with the vampires?
8. __ Have you enlisted energy buddies?
9. __ Are you open to learning from failure?
10. __ Do you know when to quit?
11. __ Do you have a system to get you through?
12. __ Does doing this give you good energy?
13. __ Do you have positive, powerful stories to tell?
14. __ Are you ready to counter your ANTs?
15. __ Do you have a plan?
16. __ Do you have the right tools?
17. __ Are you getting enough sleep?
18. __ Are you hydrated?
19. __ Is the timing right?
20. __ Can you overcome the Lie of Time?

# Appendix II

## The Riddle of Randonneuring: More Than You Want to Know about Long Distance Cycling

— — — — — — — — — — — — — — — — —

**"Nothing compares to the simple pleasure of riding a bike." —John F. Kennedy**

— — — — — — — — — — — — — — — — —

TO THE UNINITIATED (WHICH IS PROBABLY YOU IF YOU ARE READING this appendix), long distance cycling makes even less sense than running marathons. And running marathons is *crazy*.

Since long distance cycling is probably the central metaphor of this book, I want to share a few ideas about the sport.

### A Uniquely Efficient Machine

*First*, because of the unique high energy efficiency of the bicycle, it's possible to ride a *loooong* way. In short, it's possible to *live* on a bicycle for days, traveling hundreds of miles.

Early in the history of this simple machine, its ability to transport riders further than any other means, even horses, captured the imagination of its devotees. It still does. The bicycle tells its owner: *you can go farther than you think.* It is an incredibly powerful energy message. Those of us who listen to it are unceasingly surprised by what it—we—can do.

Of course, modern high-end bicycles are a far cry from the Schwinn your dad bought you as a kid. They are built of aerospace materials and engineered with the precision of medical equipment. It's easy to spend north of $10,000 on one.

## Managing Our Energy—Together

*Second,* a long distance cyclist must overcome obstacles ranging from hills and wind to flat tires and pot holes—to say nothing of other competitors for the road like SUVs and semis. These add a randomness to the sport that is often missing from tracks and swimming pools. Cyclists' ability to manage their energy through these challenges and gifts (there are downhills and tailwinds, too) is the key factor determining their success or failure.

These make cycling both an individual and a group sport. Yes, you must pedal your own bike. But draft behind a friend and the wind abates a bit. A tire change goes more quickly with a buddy helping. Almost always, riding with a teammate is easer than riding alone. It's like life.

## Randonneuring's Strange Spice

*Third,* Randonneuring is one rather strange flavor of long-distance cycling. Although it's advertised as non-competitive, it retains many elements of racing: your time is recorded and you have a limited amount of time to finish a given distance. Usually, the distance is 200 kilometers (about 125 miles) to 1200 kilometers (about 750 miles), although I have ridden events that are as short as 100 kilometers (about 62 miles) or as long as 1600 kilometers (1000 miles). Unlike racing, though, you can get a medal just for finishing—and it's the same medal no matter what place you finish. There are no special awards for the "winner," discretely referred to as the "first finisher."

Invented by the French, Randonneuring can be every bit as challenging as racing, but in a different way. Randonneuring is a ride-night-and-day, no-matter-what-the-weather, self-supported version of cycling that hails back to the early days of racing. Back then, there was no caravan of following cars to hand you a new bike if yours broke. (In fact, one legendary Tour de France racer was disqualified when he received help from a blacksmith to repair the rider's broken bike.)

## The World's Oldest Bike Race

The ultimate Randonneuring event, Paris-Brest-Paris, began as a race in 1891. Today, it continues as the Olympics of the sport, drawing thousands to Paris every four years. Although many of the riders are just hoping to finish within the 90-hour time limit for the 1200 kilometers from Paris to Brest and back, the first few riders are unquestionably racing—just as they did in the 19th Century. These "first finishers" commonly complete 750 miles in well under two days.

To me, Randonneuring is just a kinder, gentler version of racing. Many of the riders I know try to finish about as fast as they can. Nonetheless, this often means that if a friend breaks a chain or flats a tire, I will stop to help him or her. In "real" bicycle racing, that's unthinkable.

Equally unthinkable, for most bike racers, are the Randonneuring distances. For most cyclists—even fairly serious ones—100 miles is a very, very long way to go. For a Randonneur, that's a routine spin. Not surprisingly, Randonneuring tends to be an older rider's sport. They are the folks with the time to train for extreme distances. What's more, they long ago lost the fast-twitch muscles that power younger, faster riders.

For we old, gray and pokey Randonneurs, however, the answer to the riddle of why we take on the challenge of the long, long road is the same as Hillary's for Everest: "Because it's there."

— — — — — — — — — — — — — —

**Get a bicycle. You will certainly not regret it, if you live. —Mark Twain**

— — — — — — — — — — — — — —

*For more detail about long distance cycling, including Greg's cross-country diary, riding tips and videos, see his website: www. MorePersonalEnergy.com.*

# Notes

## Chapter 1

1. The Gallup Organization found that, in 2014, almost 70% of U.S. workers were not engaged in their jobs.

## Chapter 2

1. For more detail about the ride, including Greg's cross-country diary, riding tips and videos, see his website: www.MorePersonalEnergy.com.
3. Rainer Maria Rilke, trans. Joan M. Burnham, *Letters to a Young Poet*, p. 35, as quoted in *Richard Rohr's Daily Meditations*, March 5, 2016.

## Chapter 5

1. "Consumers use smart phones for 195 minutes per day," analysismason.com, May 2, 2014
2. "What's Your Fool's Gold?" Timmaurer.com, October 10, 2014
3. Red Bull is the evil animal vanquished by the Unicorn in *The Last Unicorn*. It's also the name of a popular energy drink. Coincidence? I don't think so.

## Chapter 6

1. Dollar sales of energy drink beverages and shots in the United States from 2011 to 2015 (in billion U.S. dollars). Statistica.com
2. "Top Selling Energy Drink Brands" September 5, 2104
3. "The Longest Ride: Betsy Andreu Says Faith Fueled Her Fight Against Doping Lies and Lance Armstrong," *The Detroit Free Press*, February 2, 2014
4. January 26, 2015. See www.BBC.com

## Chapter 7

1. "102-year old Robert Marchand beats own hour record," *Cycling News*, February 3, 2014
2. *An investigation into the relationship between age and physiological function in highly active older adults, January 6, 2015*
3. "How Exercise Keeps Us Young," *New York Times*, January 7, 2105
4. Lara B, Salinero J, Del Coso J. *The relationship between age and running time in elite marathoners is U-shaped. Age.* 2014.
5. Knechtle, D, et al, *Relationship between age and elite marathon race time in world single age records from 5 to 93 years.* July 31, 2014

## Chapter 8

1. A form of semi-competitive ultra-long-distance cycling. See fuller discussion of this strange sport in the Appendix.

## Chapter 9

1. One of my clients, The Shelter Group, uses "SPICE"—Spiritual, Physical, Intellectual, Cultural, Emotional.
2. See: *The Perfect Mile*

## Chapter 10

1. The concept of an "energy sink" grew out of the use of "heat sinks" on computer chips. The heat sinks prevent computers from overheating by drawing off heat energy from the devices. Sinks can be great for microprocessors... not so good for you and me.
2. See: www.sweetpoison.com
3. Wikipedia.org: "The Composition of the Human Body"

## Chapter 11

1. "In U.S., 40% Get Less Than Recommended Amount of Sleep." Gallup.com, December 19, 2013
2. For more detail about his rides, including Greg's cross-country diary, riding tips and videos, see his website: www.MorePersonalEnergy.com.
3. "One more reason to get a good night's sleep." TED talk Oct 13, 2014.
4. NASA study, *Brain Rules* Page 160
5. *Brain Rules*, p 164.
6. *Archives of Disease in Childhood,* November 2006

## Chapter 12

1. For example, in 2015 I did 35 rides of 100 miles or more in a day—and a couple over 200.
2. Wikipedia: "Alexis Lemaire"
3. *Strengthening Your Work Skills*, p 28

## Chapter 13

1. For more detail about long distance bicycling, including Greg's cross-country diary, riding tips and videos, see his website: www.MorePersonalEnergy.com.

## Chapter 14

1. https://www.ted.com/talks/david_grady_how_to_save_the_world_or_at_least_yourself_from_bad_meetings?language=en

# Chapter 15

1. In his book about the 1996 Everest tragedy, *Into Thin Air*, Jon Krakauer said climbers drank a gallon of water a day—and still dehydrated.
2. See: *How the Mighty Fall and Why Some Companies Never Give In*
3. Pages 206–208.
4. See *The Power of Story* page 28

# Chapter 16

1. ESPN SportsCenter, March 20, 2011. See: www.youtube.com/watch?v=7jATSSgWg-M
2. See: https://sites.google.com/site/bicyclehelmetmythsandfacts/ and http://www.bhsi.org/shouldi.htm
3. Richard Rohr's Daily Meditation, February 18, 2016
4. See Change Your Brain Change Your Life, page 229

# Chapter 17

1. Jay Unger and the Molly Mason Family Band
2. See: "Fearless Fosbury Flops to Glory," *The New York Times* October 20, 1968
3. For more detail about long distance bicycling, including Greg's cross-country diary, riding tips and videos, see his website: www.MorePersonalEnergy.com.
4. For more detail about long distance bicycling, including Greg's cross-country diary, riding tips and videos, see his website: www.MorePersonalEnergy.com.

# Chapter 18

1. Del Close, David Alger and others.
2. The-golf-experience.com. "Jack Nicklaus Quotes"

# Chapter 19

1. For more detail about long distance cycling, including Greg's cross-country diary, riding tips and videos, see his website: www.MorePersonalEnergy.com.
2. For more practical tips on riding across the country, see www.MorePersonalEnergy.com, and check out my cross country diary and videos.

# Chapter 20

1. *Member Handbook, 5th Edition*, Randonneurs USA, 2014
2. Page 43
3. See Dan Pink's *Drive: The Surprising Trust About What Motivates Us*
4. According to Dentist Nicholas Calcaterra in his "Directions in Destiny" Blog, the term originated during the Civil War, when soldiers needed "four front teeth" in order to tear open paper cartridges and load their guns.
5. Page 140

## Chapter 22

1. For more detail about long distance cycling, including Greg's cross-country diary, riding tips and videos, see his website: www.MorePersonalEnergy.com.
2. Pages 79–82

## Chapter 23

1. *Authentic Happiness*
2. Randy is an outstanding rider who would later complete Race Across America successfully.
3. *Harvard Business Review* Blog December 16, 2014

## Chapter 24

1. See: TED talks: "Positive Psychology" July 21, 2008
2. Chapter 11, Page 199 ff

## Chapter 25

1. Page 123

## Chapter 26

1. See Youtube: www.youtube.com/watch?v=zut2NLMVL_k

## Chapter 27

1. Frank Ryan and Greg Conderacci do a joint training, *Extraordinary Endurance: Leadership Lessons from the Long Road.* For more information, see Greg's website: www.MorePersonalEnergy.com.

## Chapter 29

1. January 28, 2016 blog.

## Chapter 30

1. *Blind Spots*, page 122
2. September 13, 2013 Blog

## Chapter 31

1. See: *Ultramarathon Man*, Page 90

## Chapter 35

1. *Antifragile: Things That Gain from Disorder*
1. Pages 127-128.

## Chapter 36

1. As quoted in *To Be Just Is to Love: Homilies for a Church Renewing* by Walter J. Burghardt, p. 214

## Chapter 37

1. Page 16

## Chapter 38

1. For more information about Greg's training on leadership, mission and energy, see his website: www.MorePersonalEnergy.com.

## Chapter 39

1. See: https://www.ted.com/talks/pico_iyer_the_art_of_stillness?language=en

# Bibliography

Adams, Scott, *How to Fail at Almost Everything and Still Win Big, Kind of the Story of My Life*. New York: Penguin, 2013

Amen, Daniel G. *Change Your Brain Change Your Life; The Breakthrough Program for Conquering Anxiety, Depression, Obsessiveness, Anger and Impulsiveness*. New York: Three Rivers Press, 1998

Amen, Daniel G. *Making a Good Brain Great: The Amen Clinic Program for Achieving and Sustaining Optimal Mental Performance*. New York: Three Rivers Press, 2005

Amen, Daniel G. *Sex on the Brain: 12 Lessons to Enhance Your Love Life*. New York: Three Rivers Press, 2007

Armstrong, Lance and Carmichael, Chris. *The Lance Armstrong Performance Program: The Training, Strengthening and Eating Plan Behind the World's Greatest Cycling Victory*. New York: Rodale, 2006.

Armstrong, Lance with Jenkins, Sally. *It's Not About the Bike: My Journey Back to Life*. New York: J. P. Putnam's, 2000

Bannister, Roger. *The Four-Minute Mile, 50th Anniversary Edition*. Guilford, CT: The Lyons Press, 2004

Bascomb, Neal. *The Perfect Mile: Three Athletes, One Goal and Less Than Four Minutes to Achieve It*. Boston: Houghton Mifflin, 2004

Bazerman, Max and Tenbrunsel, Ann. *Blind Spots: Why We Fail to Do What's Right and What to Do About It*. Princeton: Princeton University Press, 2011

Berman, Mark. *Strengthening Your Work Skills Through Personal Energy Management*.

Bolles, Richard Nelson, *What Color is Your Parachute: A Practical Manual for Job-Hunters & Career Changers*. Berkeley: 10 Speed Press, 1970

Boukreev, Anatoli. *Above the Clouds: Diaries of a High-Altitude Mountaineer.* New York: St. Martins' Griffin, 2001

Brosmer, Robert J and Waldron, Deborah. *Health & High Performance: The Total Approach to Success Through Fitness.* Dubuque, Iowa: Kendal/Hunt Publishing, 1991

Brown, Jeff and Fenske, Mark. *In The Winner's Brain: 8 Strategies Great Minds Use to Achieve Success.* Cambridge, MA; Da Capo Press, 2010

Collins, Jim. Good to Great: *Why Some Companies Make the Leap and Others Don't.* New York: HarperCollins, 2001

Collins, Jim. *How the Mighty Fall and Why Some Companies Never Give In.* New York: HarperCollins, 2009

Colvin, Geoff. *Talent Is Overrated: What Really Separates World-Class Performers from Everybody Else.* New York: Penguin, 2008

Csikszntmihalyi, Mihaly, *Flow: The Psychology of Optimal Experience.* New York: Harper & Row, 1990

Csikszntmihalyi, Mihaly, *Good Business: Leadership, Flow and the Making of Meaning.* New York: Penguin, 2003

Duhigg, Charles. *The Power of Habit: Why We Do What We Do In Life and Business.* New York: Random House, 2012

Epstein, David. *The Sports Gene: Inside the Science of Extraordinary Athletic Performance.* New York: Penguin Group, 2013

Fey, Tina. *Bossypants.* New York: Little Brown, 2011.

Frederickson, Barbara. *Positivity: Top-Notch Research Reveals the 3-to-1 Ratio That Will Change Your Life.* New York; Three Rivers Press, 2009

Gibran, Kahlil. *The Prophet.* London: Knopf, 1923

Gladwell, Malcolm. *Blink: The Power of Thinking Without Thinking.* New York: Little Brown, 2005

Gladwell, Malcolm. *David and Goliath: Underdogs, Misfits and the Art of Battling Giants.* New York: Little Brown, 2013

Gladwell, Malcolm. *Outliers: The Story of Success*. New York: Little Brown, 2008

Goodwin, Doris Kearns. *Team of Rivals: The Political Genius of Abraham Lincoln*. New York: Simon & Schuster, 2005

Gordon, Jon. *The 10 Minute Energy Solution, A Proven Plan to Increase Your Energy, Reduce Your Stress and Transform Your Life*. New York: G. P. Putnam, 2006

Haidt, Jonathan. *The Righteous Mind: Why Good People Are Divided by Politics and Religion*. New York: Pantheon, 2012

Headquarters, Department of the Army, *Survival: Department of the Army Field Manual FM21-76*. Washington, DC. 1970

Iyer, Pico. *The Art of Stillness: Adventures in Going Nowhere*. New York: Simon & Schuster, 2014

Jackson, Susan and Csikszntmihalyi, Mihaly. *Flow in Sports: The Keys to Optimal Experiences and Performances*. Champaign, IL: Human Kinetics, 1999

Kahneman, Daniel. *Thinking, Fast and Slow*. New York: Farrar, Straus and Giroux, 2011

Karnazes, Dean. *Ultramarathon Man: Confessions of an All-Night Runner*. New York: Penguin, 2005

Kearns, Brad. *How Lance Does It: Put the Success Formula of a Champion into Everything You Do*. New York: McGraw Hill, 2007

Kegan, Robert and Lahey, isa Laskow, *Immunity to Change: How to Overcome It and Unlock the Potential in Yourself and Your Organization*. Boston: Harvard Business School Publishing, 2009

Krakeuer, Jon. *Into Thin Air: A Personal Account of the Mt. Everest Disaster*. New York: Anchor, 1997

Loehr, Jim and Schwartz, Tony. *The Power of Full Engagement, Managing Energy, Not Time, Is the Key to High Performance and Personal Renewal*. New York: Simon & Schuster, 2003.

Loehr, Jim. *The Power of Story: Rewrite Your Destiny in Business and Life.* New York: Simon & Schuster, 2007.

McDougall, Christopher. *Born to Run: A Hidden Tribe, Superathletes, and the Greatest Race the World Has Never Seen.* New York: Knopf, 2009

Medina, John. *Brain Rules: 12 Principles for Surviving and Thriving at Work, Home and School.* Seattle: Pear Press, 2008

Morrell, Margot and Capparell, Stephanie. *Shakelton's Way: Leadership Lessons from the Great Antarctic Explorer.* New York: Viking, 2001

Pink, Daniel. *Drive: The Surprising Truth About What Motivates Us.* New York: Riverhead Books, 2009

Quinn, Robert. *Building the Bridge As You Walk On It: A Guide for Leading Change.* San Francisco: Jossey-Bass, 2004

Quinn, Robert. *Change the World: How Ordinary People Can Accomplish Extraordinary Results.* San Francisco: Jossey-Bass, 1996

Quinn, Robert. *Deep Change: Discovering the Leader Within.* San Francisco: Jossey-Bass, 1996

Randonneurs USA. *Member Handbook, 5th Edition.* Raleigh, NC, 2014

Rohr, Richard. *Falling Upward: A Spirituality for the Two Halves of Life.* San Francisco: Jossey-Bass, 2011

Rosen, Robert. *Just Enough Anxiety: The Hidden Driver of Business Success.* New York: Penguin, 2008

Ryan, Francis X., *Life Lessons Learned: Amazing Stories of My Walk Across America for Children.* Baltimore: Self-Published, 2015

Schulz, Kathryn. *Being Wrong: Adventures in the Margin of Error.* New York: HarperCollins, 2010

Schwartz, Barry. *The Paradox of Choice: Why More Is Less.* New York: Harper Collins, 2004

Seligman, Martin. *Authentic Happiness: Using the New Positive Psychology to Realize Your Potential for Lasting Fulfillment.* New York: Atria, 2002

Seligman, Martin. *Flourish: A Visionary New Understanding of Happiness and Well-being.* New York: Atria, 2013

Shekerjian, Denise. *Uncommon Genius: How Great Ideas Are Born.* New York: Penguin, 1991

Strickland, Bill. *The Quotable Cyclist: Great Moments of Bicycling Wisdom, Inspiration and Humor.* New York: Breakaway Books, 1997

Taleb, Nassim Nicholas. *Antifragile: Things That Gain from Disorder.* New York: Random House, 2014.

Taleb, Nassim Nicholas. *The Black Swan: The Impact of the Highly Improbable.* New York: Random House, 2007.

Tindle, Hilary. *Up: How Positive Outlook Can Transform Our Health and Aging.* New York: Penguin Group, 2013

# About Greg Conderacci

---

FOR MORE THAN FOUR DECADES, GREG CONDERACCI, AKA "BRIGHT Hawk" in energy circles, has been using the magic of communication to help people lead happier, more productive and more rewarding lives.

When he's not on a bicycle or speaking about personal energy management, he helps organizations and teams discover and defend their *Good Ground* – the fertile market niche where their productivity peaks. In other words, his company, Good Ground Consulting LLC, helps them answer their clients' question, "Why should I trust you?"

He teaches marketing at the Johns Hopkins' Bloomberg School of Public Health and also is a Senior Fellow with the Maryland Association of CPA's Business Learning Institute.

In the 2000s, he was Director of Marketing for Deutsche Bank Alex. Brown, responsible for marketing strategy, marketing materials creation and design, and sales force coaching and training. In the 1990s, Greg was Director of Marketing for Price Waterhouse's information technology consulting practice in the Mid-Atlantic, Mid-Atlantic Vice President of Sales and Marketing for Prudential's managed care operations, and Chief Marketing Officer for Alex. Brown (America's Oldest Investment Bank).

In the 1980s, he created and marketed several innovative programs for the poor of Maryland, including the state's largest soup kitchen (it's where the Pope eats when he comes to Baltimore). In the 1970s, as a reporter for *The Wall Street Journal*, Greg covered business in Detroit (mostly autos) and also wrote economics out of Washington.

A *magna cum laude* graduate of Princeton University, he was Editor-in-Chief of *The Daily Princetonian;* he also holds a Masters in Public Policy from Harvard University. He is the proud father of two high-energy daughters.

For more information about Greg and his riding adventures, see his website: www. MorePersonalEnergy.com.

Or follow his blog, www.MorePersonalEnergy.com/blog.

# Getting UP! With Greg

Greg Conderacci offers a wide variety of **training** programs, including:

- Energy management training, presentations, motivational speeches and keynotes
- Sales training, especially around boosting productivity and performance
- Leadership training, especially around identity and motivation
- Change management training
- Business development training, including high-energy sales skills
- Presentation training
- Team building
- Professional ethics
- Writing and communication skills development

He also offers **marketing consulting**, including:

- Marketing strategy
- Message development
- Marketing planning
- Identity and positioning

As an experienced **meeting facilitator**, he can help guide:

- Strategic planning
- Marketing efforts, including events and campaigns
- Team building
- Branding and re-branding
- Tagline and message development
- Brainstorming
- Problem-solving

Greg has worked with scoress of for-profit and non-profit organizations in a variety of industries, including:

- Health care
- Professional services
- Financial services
- Social services
- Education

For more information or to contact Greg, see
**www.MorePersonalEnergy.com** or
**www.GoodGroundConsulting.com**